PREACHERS OF A DIFFERENT GOSPEL

Evang. Lizzie Johnson

PREACHERS OF A DIFFERENT GOSPEL

A Pilgrim's Reflections on Contemporary Trends in Christianity

Femi Bitrus Adeleye

Copyright © 2011 by Femi Bitrus Adeleye

Published 2011 by **HippoBooks**, an imprint of WordAlive, ACTS, Step, and Zondervan.

WordAlive Publishers, PO Box 4547, GP0-00100, Nairobi, Kenya
www.wordalivepublishers.org

Africa Christian Textbooks (ACTS), TCNN, PMB 2020, Bukuru 930008, Plateau State, Nigeria www.africachristiantextbooks.com

Step Publishers, PO Box AN 11150, Accra-North, Ghana
www.stepbooks.org

Zondervan, *Grand Rapids, Michigan 49530*
www.zondervan.com

Library of Congress Cataloging-in-Publication Data

Adeleye, Femi.
    Preachers of a different gospel : a pilgrim's reflections on contemporary trends in Christianity / Femi Bitrus Adeleye.
       p. cm.
    Originally published: Kampala, Uganda : IFES Anglophone Africa, 1999.
    Includes bibliographical references.
    ISBN 978-9-966-00315-7 (softcover)
    1. Christianity--21st century. I. Title.
BR121.3.A34 2011
270.8'3--dc22   2011006832

All rights reserved.

No part of this book may be reproduced or transmitted in any form or by any means, electronic or mechanical, including photocopying, recording or by any information storage or retrieval system without permission in writing from the publisher.

All Scripture quotations, unless otherwise indicated, are taken from the Holy Bible, *Today's New International Version*®, *TNIV*®. Copyright © 2001, 2005 by Biblica, Inc.™ Used by permission of Zondervan. All rights reserved worldwide.

Cover design: Luz Design, projectluz.com
Book design: To a Tee Ltd, www.2at.com

11 12 13 14 15 16 /DCI/ 26 25 24 23 22 21 20 19 18 17 16 15 14 13 12 11 10 9 8 7 6 5 4 3 2 1

CONTENTS

Acknowledgements.................................... vii
Abbreviations.. ix
The Gospel According to the Modern Preacher xi

1   Introduction 1
2   Strange Times, Strange Gospel...................... 5
3   Between the Cross and Champagne 15
4   Charismatic Renewal and Confusion 29
5   The "Modern" Preachers........................... 41
6   Misreading the Scriptures......................... 51
7   Counterfeit Faith................................. 61
8   The Delusions of Prosperity....................... 75
9   The God Man Uses 107
10   Phoney Christianity............................. 117
11   Authentic Christianity 129

    Notes... 143

ACKNOWLEDGEMENTS

This book has largely been the result of my own reflections as a pilgrim in interaction with people and trends within the family of God. In this continuing pilgrimage, I have not travelled alone. So I am grateful to my fellow pilgrims – friends, family members, pastors, writers, teachers, helpers and prayer partners – who have influenced my reflections in various ways or helped in the process of producing this book. I am eternally grateful to those who gave me a solid foundation in the way of the cross, among whom are Mama Mary Frank-Kirkpatrick, Harris and Neva Poole as well as Kola Ejiwunmi.

I am equally thankful to pastors and friends like Gordion Okezie, Victor Musa, Bill Leslie and Josiah Idowu-Fearon who have been of great encouragement in my own nurture as I have encountered various "gospels". Not to be left out are some friends and writers who have challenged my thinking and reflection. Notable among these are Philip Yancey, who helped me greatly in rereading Scripture to get to know Jesus and his teachings better, and Uncle John Stott, who made me know that my mind matters when it comes to the truths of God. There are also writers I have not known personally but whose research and works have helped me in producing this work; among such are Warren W. Wiersbe and Hank Hanegraaff.

I cannot but thank students and co-workers within the IFES movement with whom I have interacted on some of the contents of this book. I am equally grateful to my friend and brother, the Rt. Rev. David Zac Niringiye, now Bishop of Kampala, who has helped me to think much more about our African context than I probably would have. The same appreciation goes to my secretaries – Grace Dogo in Jos and Linah

Muchimika in Harare, who helped type the manuscripts over and over again.

Then there are others whose silent witness lack the language of contemporary spirituality but who have nevertheless been supportive. Among such are my mother and others in the family who have watched and prayed along.

The greatest appreciation, apart from that owed to God, goes to my wife, Affy, and our children, Remi, Philip, Olive-Kemi and Emmanuel, who gave me time to think and to write. Affy not only understood my withdrawal to the study, but also typed and proofread the manuscript. Our children eventually understood why I sometimes could not play soccer or do other things with them.

Finally, to God be the glory for making this book possible and for the constant reminder that Jesus is the way, and the truth and the life. No one comes to the Father except through him alone.

ABBREVIATIONS

ESV   English Standard Version
KJV   King James Version
NKJV New King James Version
NLT   New Living Translation

THE GOSPEL ACCORDING TO THE MODERN PREACHER

Strong on Pentecost ...
but weak on the cross.
Strong on celebration ...
but weak on contemplation.
Strong on rejoicing, weak on reflection; strong on vocalising, weak on meditation.

Strong on power and authority ...
but weak on submission and humility.
Strong on the place of noise and shouts ...
but weak on the role of silence in the formation of the saints.
Strong on external forms of spirituality but weak on inner renewal.

Strong on deeds ...
but weak on being.
Strong on faith ...
but weak on patience.
Strong on the gifts of the Spirit but weak on the fruit of the Spirit.

Gullible on prosperity ...
but frugal on integrity.
Gullible on possessing ...
but frugal on renouncing.
Strong on self gratification but weak on self sacrifice.

This strange gospel ...
strong on zeal but weak in knowledge and purity.
Turned from faith in God ...
to faith in faith.
Turned from trust in God to trust in man.

Did someone once say,
"Seek ye first the kingdom of God and His righteousness,
and all these things shall be added unto you"?
This strange gospel says,
"Seek ye first the riches of this world and the fullness thereof,
and the kingdom of God shall be added unto you."

1

INTRODUCTION

I grew up being taught that, "If anyone is in Christ, the new creation has come: the old has gone, the new is here" (2 Cor 5:17). The lady who led me to Christ, Mama Mary Frank-Kirkpatrick, made me understand this truth. I believed it wholeheartedly – and still do. Her simple but clear explanation of that verse was just what I needed. Even though I was only thirteen, I knew something was wrong with my ability to do right or please God. Having been brought up in a strict Baptist home, I had a good understanding of the difference between right and wrong, and desired to do right to please both God and my parents. But much of my attempt to please my mother was a failure. I knew most of what I should not do, but I kept doing it all the same. I wanted to please God and go to heaven but I realised if I could hardly please my mother by doing the right things, there was no way I could meet the standards of a righteous God. So when Mama Kirkpatrick told me Jesus was able to give me a new heart and make me a brand-new person, I was quite ready for that to happen. Her simple but clear explanation of the gospel gripped my sinful heart and brought a new light into my life. I went on to trust Jesus as my Saviour and Lord. My life was changed.

Mama Kirkpatrick also taught me that without holiness, no one shall see the Lord. I believed it wholeheartedly – and still do. All through high school, preliminary college and university, I affirmed a gospel that emphasised repentance, renewal, and Christ-likeness. We honestly sang, "Things are different now, something happened to me when I gave my life to Jesus."

That *something* was transformation. Our goal was to be like Jesus in all of our life. We were well taught and believed that, "Blessed are the pure in heart, for they will see God" (Matt 5:8). Also, "He who says he abides in him ought himself also so to walk just as he walked" (1 John 2:6).

Through the ministry of the Fellowship of Christian Students (FCS) and later the Nigeria Fellowship of Evangelical Students (NIFES), we were well-schooled in the meaning of Christian commitment and discipleship. We were also given rigorous discipleship training by Calvary Productions (CAPRO), an indigenous mission group, and by Scripture Union (SU). These were significant foundations which have remained irreplaceable.

Now, you must realise those were ancient days. These are modern days and things are quite different now. Really, really different. Let me illustrate:

An advert for an evangelistic crusade in Zaria, one of the major cities in Nigeria, read something like this:

> Are you barren? Come to Jesus,
> Are you a failure? Come to Jesus.
> Are you poor and want prosperity?
> Are all your plans not working out?
> Are you sick?
> Are you being attacked?
> Come to Jesus,
> Come and be healed.
> Claim your inheritance and prosperity.

On the surface, this appeal seems all right. But a man who examined the list of needs on the poster might decide that he didn't fit into any of those categories. He would conclude that he did not need Jesus.

But let us assume that this man went to the crusade and all the needs listed were met. What would happen then? He would have been helped to escape some of the realities of life but might remain lost in his sins. Is this evangelism? The danger is not just that the means and methods of evangelism have become cheap and commercialised but that the very heart of the gospel is being corrupted. The popular trend is that people are no longer attracted to Jesus for who he is or because they need a Saviour to save them from their sins. Rather, they are lured to Jesus for the blessings or benefits they can claim from him. Welcome to the gospel according to the modern preacher.

It is not too difficult to discern that there is a new gospel in town. Its impact is reflected in the songs sung in fellowship meetings and some churches. Several years ago, it was common to hear saved people sing,

> I have decided to follow Jesus
> I have decided to follow Jesus
> I have decided to follow Jesus
> No turning back, no turning back

Or

> If I gained the world but not the Saviour …

Songs like these have been overtaken by songs like, "I am a millionaire", or "I am a winner" and even "I shall not die".

In the past Christians sang, "With Christ in the vessel, I smile at the storm". Today, no storms are expected in a Christian's life. Life is meant to be trial-free if one is in Christ. Whereas even non-Christians sang, "This world is not my home", it is more common today to sing, "This is my Father's world, why should the devil have all the riches?"

The same difference is noticeable in the favourite memory verses of the day. Whereas verses like, "He must become greater; I must become less" (John 3:30) were once popular, today it is more popular to assert, "We shall be the head and not the tail" (Deut 28:13), even when we have not worked enough, or "We are gods" in gross misinterpretation of the context of Psalm 82:6 and John 10:34.

The shift from a Christocentric gospel to one that appeals more to the satisfaction of our immediate appetites has produced what has been described as "adulterated" or "fraudulent" Christianity. It has also been called a "fluffy" or "cross-less" gospel. One pastor bluntly calls it the gospel of greed. It is a gospel that tends to make life here on earth as convenient as possible without preparing people for eternity.

I wonder what Paul would say to our generation when so long ago he told the Galatians:

> I am astonished that you are so quickly deserting the one who called you by the grace of Christ and are turning to a different gospel – which is really no gospel at all. Evidently some people are throwing you into confusion and are trying to pervert

> the gospel of Christ. But even if we or an angel from heaven should preach a gospel other than the one we preached to you, let that person be under God's curse! (Gal 1:6–8)

The days we live in demand that we not only take these words seriously but also examine ourselves to know if we are still in the faith or not. We are surrounded on all sides by preachers of a different gospel who twist the word of God to suit their desired ends. By manipulating the Bible, they distort the gospel of our Lord Jesus Christ and mislead those who are not careful enough to see through their deceit.

Our task in this book is not to criticise or judge anyone or any group of persons. Rather, it is to examine the claims of various shades of this different gospel in the light of Scripture and expose what contradicts the essence of biblical faith. It is also to warn those who may not be aware of the subtle ways in which false teaching has crept into the church. It is almost impossible to expose these trends without mentioning specific names, and so this has been done when necessary, not with the motive of judging but to expose teachings that are not consistent with the gospel as it was once entrusted to the saints.

2

STRANGE TIMES, STRANGE GOSPEL

The Spirit clearly says that in later times some will abandon the faith and follow deceiving spirits and things taught by demons. Such teachings come through hypocritical liars, whose consciences have been seared as with a hot iron.

— 1 Timothy 4:1–2

But mark this: There will be terrible times in the last days. People will be lovers of themselves, lovers of money, boastful, proud, abusive, disobedient to their parents, ungrateful, unholy, without love, unforgiving, slanderous, without self-control, brutal, not lovers of the good, treacherous, rash, conceited, lovers of pleasure rather than lovers of God – having a form of godliness but denying its power. Have nothing to do with such people.

— 2 Timothy 3:1–5

The times that the Apostle Paul warned about in the above passages have certainly come upon us. Events and trends within the church and in society are sufficient evidence that we do live in dangerous times. These are times in which it is becoming more difficult to differentiate between faith and fantasy, and between devotion to Christ and religious delusion. We live in times when the line between churches and cults is thin and people easily mistake spiritism for spirituality. These are strange times indeed. Times when people wholeheartedly follow strange teachings and philosophies even within the church; times of strong addiction to seducing spirits; and times when leaders feed their flock with false doctrines. As regards the content and practice of the gospel, only those with discernment, who understand the times and refuse to compromise their vision, know the difference between the true and the counterfeit gospel.

Strange Times

These are times when sin is being redefined so that the things that used to be sin are no longer considered sinful. I have wondered whether the admonition by many a preacher to the faithful to "claim your inheritance of prosperity" is not just spiritualising covetousness. These are days of confusion in which the doors of the church are wide open to worldly values and standards. The result is a confusing mix of worldly holiness and holy worldliness. Worldly holiness is the commitment of a people meant to be holy to worldly standards. This is to say that men and women who are created in the image of God have seriously embraced the world and yet feel comfortable with both being "holy" and clinging to values that contradict that attribute. Holy worldliness is when worldly things are "sanctified" and called holy and the worldly claim to be born again simply because of their external affiliations. In other words, those who are yet to have an encounter with Christ or be transformed by him now commonly claim allegiance to him by clothing their worldliness in "spiritual" garb when it is convenient to do so.

Strange times indeed! Times when one can be "born again" and not be a new creature in Christ. Times when one can claim to be "spiritual" and yet show no evidence of this in one's character, conduct, value system, relationships or lifestyle.

These are days in which clear truths from Scripture are considered outdated and new revelations and experiences are sought with all gullibility. Some of these trends are being perpetrated by undisciplined young converts who claim they know more than Scripture reveals. These are days of lying wonders in which teachers who make miracles an end in themselves lead astray those who want a miracle at all costs. These are days when the gospel has come to be viewed as a short cut to the good things of life – a good car or a bigger house. This strange gospel promises entertainment without commitment, and those who embrace it are content to accumulate titles at the expense of a good testimony. For the love of celebration we have shifted from the "great commission" to the "great entertainment". The attraction of this mixture of worldly religion and the gospel is so strong that believers are being seduced by it.

It is a time when the church tends to listen much more to the world than to the *word*. Too many people who claim to be Christians seem to agree when the world declares that sin is harmless and godliness is not only harmful but also dangerous to good living. Current events and modern lifestyles are pressurising the church into believing that God is either tired of running his world or that his word is no longer relevant. So human beings play God and in the process make a total mess of both themselves and the world. And those who want to keep pace both with the world and with God have ended up being seduced to embrace strong religious delusions: "Just as they did not think it worthwhile to retain the knowledge of God, so God gave them over to a depraved mind, so that they do what ought not to be done" (Rom 1:28).

The real tragedy is that this mindset has crept into the church, with the result that the church itself has become worldlier. Just as Lot's association with Sodom and Gomorrah (and tolerance of their values) cost him his sense of spiritual discernment, this conformity to the world takes away the Christian's sense of right and wrong. Hence our understanding of Christian values is as blurred as our discernment of the difference between clean and unclean, true and false or holy and unholy. Like salt that has lost its flavour, we have almost altogether lost our relevance in society. As Warren W. Wiersbe puts it:

> For nineteen centuries, the church has been telling the world to admit its sins, repent and believe the gospel. Today, in the light of the twentieth century, the world is telling the church to face up to her sins, repent, and start being the true church of the gospel.[1]

Even the world knows that all is not well in the church. It is no longer uncommon for the secular media to call the church to order and challenge church leaders to be true to Jesus Christ. This is clearly a role reversal – the world is rebuking the church.

Strange Christians

What these trends have done is confront us with a generation of Christians whose lifestyle is different from that which Christ taught, Christians who have departed from the simplicity of Christ. We are left with a generation of Christians who explain away their shortcomings with a new understanding of Scripture, a new teaching or a new revelation. Whereas older generation Christians talk of honesty, integrity, character and the fruit of the Holy Spirit as essential marks of a Christian, we are being made to believe today that the mark of a Christian is the ability to be slain in the spirit or to have instant results by the use of deified objects like anointing oil.

Furthermore, we have a generation of Christians who have lost a sense of awe in the presence of God. The new breed of Christians, with the Internet pace of today's world, have little patience with waiting on God. This generation of Christians believe in "sweat-less victory" and instant results without pain. Yet, the making of a man or woman of God still takes as much time as the unchanging God has always desired. It cannot be made instant by the speed-driven pace of the contemporary world. Busy with our activities and entertainment, the words of an anonymous saint remain true: "If the Spirit of God were to leave the earth today, 90% of all Christian ministry would still continue unaffected."

One of the greatest losses in the church today is the emphasis on repentance. We have replaced a gospel that emphasised contrition and repentance with one that indulges our "self-esteem" or offers us deliverance services when our urgent need is to repent. How have some of us come to believe that the remedy for outward expression of a fallen sinful nature is a dose of deliverance service rather than repentance? Even those who have yet to encounter Christ in a personal way are herded to the altar of deliverance as if their sinful nature only needs a little trimming for their inward good to be released. How far we have drifted from the words of Oswald Chambers:

> The entrance into the Kingdom is through the pains of repentance, crashing into a man's respectable goodness; then the Holy Ghost, who produces these agonies, begins the formation of the Son of God in the life. The new life

will manifest itself in conscious repentance and unconscious holiness, never the other way round. The bedrock of Christianity is repentance. Strictly speaking, a man cannot repent when he chooses; repentance is a gift of God. The old puritans used to pray for "the gift of tears". If ever you cease to know the virtue of repentance, you are in darkness.²

Scripture remains true, "He who has the Son has life; he who does not have the Son of God does not have life" (1 John 5:12).

Strange Gospel

The root of this pathetic situation is the departure of a significant part of the church from the gospel that was once entrusted to the saints. What the church believes determines what the church practices. Wrong teaching always produces a wrong lifestyle. As flies follow infested sores, so degenerate conduct follows false beliefs. Therefore when the word of God is twisted or manipulated to accommodate various forms of subjective interests, it ceases to be "the power of God that brings salvation" (Rom 1:16). It is only the truth of God as God intends it to be interpreted that remains the power of God that brings salvation. Jesus did not stop at asking the expert in the law what is written in the law. He also asked, "How do you read it?" (Luke 10:26).

The way we interpret or misinterpret the word of God determines what we believe or practise. The misinterpretation of the word of God to back a new revelation or word of knowledge is to be resisted by all who desire to live godly lives in Christ Jesus. Paul, writing to Timothy, warns:

> Guard what has been entrusted to your care. Turn away from godless chatter and the opposing ideas of what is falsely called knowledge, which some have professed and in so doing have departed from the faith. (1 Tim 6:20–21)

Most African countries have a rich Christian heritage from the labours of the pioneering missionaries and the early recipients of the gospel they proclaimed. From the early witness of David Livingstone (who travelled thousands of miles on foot in East Africa to spread the gospel) to the impact of Mary Slessor of Calabar (the Scottish missionary who ended the slaughter of twin children in south-eastern Nigeria), most countries have rich accounts of missionary exploits. Many of these missionaries died from malaria and other hazards of the continent. Missionaries have their faults, as do we all, but it is ingratitude to lump all their efforts together with the negative aspects of Western colonialism. The many schools, hospitals and agricultural projects initiated by these missionaries led to the emancipation of our people and the development of our nations.

Beyond these, they are perhaps best remembered for the simple gospel they preached. It was the basic gospel of humanity's fallen nature and our inability to save ourselves; of God's wonderful love and intervention to save us through his only begotten Son, Jesus Christ; and the free gift of salvation for all who believe. It was so simple and uncomplicated, yet powerful. It was that basic gospel that gave birth to the revival that swept through most of East Africa for several decades and saw the growth of indigenous churches across the continent. Today, thanks to these pioneering efforts, the land that was once called the "Dark Continent" is where the church is perhaps experiencing the fastest growth.

This same continent that received such a rich gospel is now the land of a gospel that has become increasingly complicated. Our continent has become famous as the dumping ground for the refuse of the world. From used clothes to toxic waste, Africa has become a home for all forms of junk. And we readily buy them all – second-hand shoes and underwear, third-hand vehicles and aircraft, as well as all the junk manufactured in Hollywood. In the same way we gullibly embrace all forms of strange doctrines manufactured in other parts of the world, polish them a bit or mix them with indigenous flavourings, and we are set for the new gospel according to the "modern preacher". This revised gospel in all its distorted forms is a threat to the foundation laid by the original brand of missionaries. When a little truth is overemphasised or de-emphasised, it is easy to cling to half-truths or blatant untruths.

Beyond Africa, the church worldwide faces the challenge of perverted doctrine. From North America to South Asia and from Latin America to Eastern Europe, the challenge is the same. The distortion and misinterpretation of Scripture has increasingly compromised biblical truth and produced a church drifting more and more towards the values of popular celebrity culture. We must take seriously the warning of the Apostles.

Be Warned

The letter of Jude was written primarily to warn us about the threat of false doctrine and urge us to remain faithful to biblical teaching. Jude wrote:

> Dear friends, although I was very eager to write to you about the salvation we share, I felt compelled to write and urge you to contend for the faith that the Lord has once for all entrusted to us, his people. (Jude 3)

Jude, the brother of Christ, knew what he was talking about. He wrote primarily to believers whom he referred to as "those called", "loved" and "kept". He urged them to "contend for the faith" or the body of truths taught by the Apostles. These Apostles were the eyewitnesses of Jesus. They had walked with him, listened to him and were direct witnesses to all he did. To "contend" is to "stand for" or "hold fast to". It is to defend it against heresies and apostasy. His use of "once for all" to describe the faith indicates that it was completely given and is not to be added to or subtracted from. The body of truth was entrusted to the Apostles and it is our privilege to share in it. This great privilege also comes with the responsibility of jealously guarding it against distortions.

Why did Jude write this? It is because he knew that godless people would creep into the church, as they did even in his days (v. 4). These godless people would pervert the grace of God and turn it into a licence to do anything they wanted. They would go so far as to deny the Lordship of Christ by their words and lifestyle. They would do this by distorting the truths of God.

Jude gives examples of people who deviated from God's word and what happened to them. There was the tragic fate of many of those who were delivered from Egypt but still perished in the wilderness because of their unbelief, the fate of the angels who were destroyed, and the fate of Sodom and Gomorrah (vs. 5–7).

Jude's words deserve serious consideration. We are witnesses to these realities in the church today. The church has been invaded by false teachers and seducing spirits. Some doctrines taught from pulpits that were once sacred (and from newly established ones) are nothing less than doctrines of demons.

How should we respond in the light of the trends of our time? Jude says very clearly:

> But, dear friends, remember what the apostles of our Lord Jesus Christ foretold. They said to you, "In the last times, there will be scoffers who will follow their own ungodly desires." (Jude 17–18)

We must always remember these warnings and take them seriously. We must refuse to walk in the ways of the ungodly, or stand in the way of sinners, or sit in the seat of scoffers (Ps 1:1). Many of those who teach false things or distort the truths of God do so to satisfy their ungodly desires. Rather than follow them, we must build ourselves up in our most holy faith and be on our guard by praying in the Holy Spirit. To build ourselves up in our most holy faith is to pursue personal edification and renewal through an intimate relationship with God and obedience to his word. To pray in the Holy Spirit is not just to pray in tongues but to pray out of a heart indwelt by and filled with the Holy Spirit. Then we must keep ourselves within the boundaries where God's love can reach us. As we do this, it should be with the expectation of the Lord's return, for "those who have this hope purify themselves" (1 John 3:3).

There are at least eight key commands from the short book of Jude that are worth remembering:

(i) Contend for the faith (v. 3).
(ii) Remember what the apostles of our Lord Jesus Christ foretold (v. 17).
(iii) Build yourselves up in your most holy faith (v. 20).
(iv) Pray in the Holy Spirit (v. 20).
(v) Keep yourselves in God's love (v. 21).
(vi) Wait for the mercy of our Lord Jesus Christ to bring you to eternal life (v. 21).

(vii) Be merciful to those who doubt, save others by snatching them from the fire. to others show mercy, mixed with fear (v. 22–23).
(viii) Hate even the clothing stained by corrupted flesh (v. 23).

Finally, remember that we are not saved by our own efforts. It is God who keeps us from falling into error as we cooperate with him, and he preserves us eternally. God is able to give us complete victory over false teaching when we turn to him. Hence Jude completes his letter by saying:

> To him who is able to keep you from stumbling and to present you before his glorious presence without fault and with great joy – to the only God our Saviour be glory, majesty, power and authority, through Jesus Christ our Lord, before all ages, now and forevermore! Amen. (Jude 24–25)

3

BETWEEN THE CROSS AND CHAMPAGNE

Christ calls men to carry a cross; we call them to have fun in His name. He calls them to forsake the world; we assure them that if they but accept Jesus the world is their oyster. He calls them to suffer; we call them to enjoy all the bourgeois comforts modern civilization affords. He calls them to self-abnegation and death; we call them to spread themselves like green bay trees or perchance even to become stars in a pitiful fifth-rate religious zodiac. He calls them to holiness; we call them to a cheap and tawdry happiness that would have been rejected with scorn by the least of the Stoic philosophers.

— A. W. Tozer

I was once told the story of a politician appealing to his constituency as he sought re-election. He confessed to having spent his first year in office using the resources attached to his position to look after himself. He equally admitted to having spent his second year in office using the resources to cater for his business needs. In the third year, he attended to the needs of his family. It was time for elections again and people had to choose between him and another candidate. Having given an account of his self-centred first term in office, our politician friend warned his people that his opponent, if elected to replace him, was likely to spend his first term in office in the same way. However, since he had attended to his personal, business and family needs in his first term, he was now ready to use his second term in office to attend to the needs of his constituency. He warned that if they elected his opponent they would have to wait many more years to benefit from anything.

For some, such choices are matters of life and death. We have a much more serious choice before us today. A choice that is actually a matter of life and death – it is the choice between the gospel of the cross and the "gospel of champagne" as I call it.

Once upon a Gospel

In 1975 a fellow student called Bitrus watched as a wealthy man mistakenly dropped a naira bill on the ground. Bitrus' initial response was to call the man's attention to the money and return it to him. But instead he waited until the man moved away. He then ran to pick up the money and pocketed it, dreaming of several things he could do with it.

That night as he knelt down to pray, Bitrus could not pray. His mind was on the money and an inner voice told him clearly that he had stolen it. Try as he would, he could not pray. You see, Bitrus had committed his life to Christ some years earlier and knew that what he had done was wrong. Yet he felt he needed the money, so he kept it. Meanwhile the man who dropped the money travelled back to his town several miles away.

For about two weeks, Bitrus wrestled with his conscience. One day he came to terms with what to do. He repented of having kept the money and took action, travelling to see the owner of the money and confess how he had sinned by picking it and keeping it. The surprised owner of the money wondered why Bitrus should have travelled so far to return something he had not even noticed was missing. He told Bitrus to keep the money but Bitrus refused, saying that would be displeasing to the Lord. Having returned the money, he felt clean and returned to school rejoicing. Bitrus knew that he could not be a Christian and live with sin; he had received the gospel that emphasised newness of life and abstinence from all appearance of evil.

I remember another student who gained admission to the university by cheating in an exam. When he became a Christian, he repented and admitted his offence to the university authorities. As a result, he suffered the loss of a year in school but was glad to have done so.

Such stories were common during our student days – new Christians repented and returned things they had stolen or went back to admit lies they had told. For although there were spectacular conversion experiences, the main emphasis was on the complete turning away from sin that resulted from receiving Jesus as Saviour and Lord. Restitution was encouraged as a mark of repentance. Students who had stolen library books returned them with apologies. People who had been dishonest went back to confess their sins and make things right. Some did exactly what Zacchaeus did, repaying much more than they had taken unlawfully.

There were several accounts of revivals. The 1972 revivals in Gindiri, a small town in Northern Nigeria, were characterised by genuine repentance, all-night prayers, confessions of hatred, drunkenness, possession of stolen goods and so forth.[1] The East African Revival involved such things as testimonies and confessions from those who killed husbands during the Mau Mau uprisings in Kenya. Christians were both feared and respected in society! There was fear of committing public or secret sins.

There was nothing unusual about these stories in the 1970s in Nigeria. Rather they were common because that was part of what it meant to be Christian. That was a period when there were fresh winds of revival and new life in the church. The preaching of the gospel transformed lives in schools, churches and some parts of society. This is what it meant for many in my country in the 1970s to be Christians. It was not seen as a call to an easy life. There was an emphasis on the cross of Christ and on willingness to suffer for Christ if need be. It was also common to be taught that, *"Everyone who wants to live a godly life in Christ Jesus will be persecuted"* (2 Tim 3:12, emphasis mine). It was common to sing:

> It's not an easy road we are trav'lling to Heaven,
> For many are the thorns on the way;
> It's not an easy road but the Saviour is with us,
> His presence gives us joy ev'ry day.[2]

Love was genuine. It was a sacrificial love that shared freely with others in need. It was a love that gave and gave, not because one expected God to return it a hundredfold but because it was right and loving to do so. I know a student who gave up all his pocket money to pay a sister's school fees so she would not be thrown out of school. Relationships were transparent, governed by honesty and concern for the other person's interest such that it was almost like the accounts in the Acts of the Apostles. There was much emphasis on the fruit of the Holy Spirit: love, joy, peace, long-suffering etc. (Gal 5:22–25). You didn't need to teach anyone about humility – conversion was so thorough that humility simply flowed out.

In addition to all these, there was fervent evangelistic zeal in all who were truly saved. The eagerness to share the gospel was irrepressible. There was door-to-door evangelism, open-air crusades, prison and hospital evangelism. Students got on trains and buses and taxis not because they needed to travel but for the sole purpose of witnessing to travellers. They were like an army let loose to turn the world right side up by their lives and vocal witness. They loftily sang, "You shall be my witnesses … in Jerusalem, in Samaria, and to the uttermost parts of the world."

As I look back, I wonder what it was that made the difference. There was obviously a move of God. Added to this was the content of what was preached as the gospel. There was a strong emphasis on the gospel being the power of God unto salvation. Salvation meant a personal encounter with Jesus Christ and a life committed to following him wholeheartedly regardless of the cost. The gospel of the day was a gospel of the cross. The underlying theology was a call to take up the cross and follow Jesus. It was to turn one's back on the world and all its values and follow Christ. The old Scripture Union song sums it up:

> The world behind me, the cross before me
> The world behind me, the cross before me
> The world behind me, the cross before me
> No turning back, no turning back.
>
> Though none goes with me, I still will follow
> Though none goes with me, I still will follow
> Though none goes with me, I still will follow
> No turning back, no turning back.

Before we examine the content of that true gospel it is needful to examine how much we have drifted.

The Gospel of Champagne

Champagne is a popular type of wine named after the region in France where it is produced. Champagne bottles are opened to celebrate achievements and at parties. It is a symbol of festivity, celebration and glamour; an appropriate representation of the notion of pleasure and the promise to escape from pain even if only for a short time.

Some drinks have a tendency to knock you out permanently. For instance, when the beer adverts proclaim, "You are brighter by far on a star", they say nothing about finding yourself in a gutter the next morning, or beating up your wife, or slamming the door in the face of your children and making them bitter for life. Nor do they warn that drunk driving may lead to an early grave. Advertisers are committed to telling only half-truths or less than the whole truth. They simply promise instant pleasure and some temporary escape from reality.

I heard of a man who drifted uninvited into a party in Nairobi. Before long he became thrilled with tasting all the drinks available. From popular beer he moved on to champagne and later something called "Vat". He soon became gifted with strange utterances and unprecedented body twisting. Not long after, he collapsed and was unconscious. Since he had drifted into the party, no one knew where he had come from or what his name was. Dead drunk, he was dragged out into the street. He remained there for a full forty-eight hours, oblivious to earthly realities. Then he woke up like a man coming back from the dead and staggered away in search of his home.

That is what the gospel of champagne does to drifters. Like those who advertise alcoholic beverages, propagators of this gospel tell only half-truths and promise short-term thrills. Whereas the gospel of the cross calls for repentance and denial of self and other things, the gospel of champagne calls for self-satisfaction in response to stimuli from diverse entertaining attractions. Whereas the way of the cross points to renunciation, forsaking of opposing values, sobriety and participation in the fellowship of Christ's sufferings, the new way, the way of champagne, calls for a lifestyle committed to gullible celebration and self-indulgence with pleasures opposed to kingdom values.

Whereas the cross points to death, champagne points to celebration. The person facing the cross is often on a lonesome journey of no return. The man facing the bottle of champagne is often in the good company of celebrants. Two thousand years ago we were told, "Happy are the sad", "Blessed are they that mourn", today we are being told by some that if you are a Christian "you will have no more sorrows, no more pains, no suffering."

Jesus said, "Whoever wants to be my disciple must deny themselves and take up their cross and follow me" (Mark 8:34). Exponents of today's gospel find that kind of saying dangerous. Such teaching will drive members away. Instead they say, "If you want to follow Jesus, reject poverty, disown all suffering, satisfy your appetites and find fulfilment." One of them has written:

> When Jesus came, he knew His commission and declared it very clearly. I say this over and over again, God sent me. He said, "Go and make my people rich!" That is an assurance that wherever I stand, poverty must not survive."[3]

He goes on to say concerning his megachurch,

> No one under this ministry is permitted to be poor, nor programmed for affliction. God told me, "Go and stop the tears of mankind." I heard Him clearly. God sent me for your financial rescue.[4]

The lure of this form of gospel and the preoccupation with the pursuit of earthly wealth and conveniences has shipwrecked the faith of many. For those who embrace this new gospel, any biblical reference to inconvenience or pain sounds rather strange. The Apostle Paul's admonition that, "everyone who wants to live a godly life in Christ Jesus will be persecuted" (2 Tim 3:12) is indeed strange for the days we live in.

Since the cross of Christ is a symbol of separation, surrender, crucifixion, and death – leading to conversion, renewal, victory, commitment and a purposeful life – this new gospel has no room for the cross or for the real Jesus of the cross. It has created a new Jesus whose primary purpose for coming into the world is to make people comfortable and guarantee their security. This Jesus is not Lord but is like the genie in the bottle, a servant to guarantee good health, wealth and pleasure. This Jesus is distant from the Jesus of Nazareth, who was given the name Jesus because he shall "save his people from their sins" (Matt 1:21) and who said, "Do not worry about your life, what you will eat or drink; or about your body, what you will wear. Is not life more important than food, and the body more important than clothes?" (Matt 6:25)

This strange gospel is producing a new generation of Christians who cannot wait until heaven to celebrate but, like the prodigal son, want maximum celebration and pleasure here and now. Some of this new generation of Christians have turned the grace of God into a licence for all manner of unrighteousness. They have abused faith and turned it from faith in God to faith in faith or faith in the "man of God" who is the commander while God is the slave who must produce whatever is demanded. Such people have been taught to give to God only with the motive of trying to manipulate God to return their gift a hundredfold.

We know something about the Sadducees of old. It is said that they were "sad" because they wanted the best of two opposing lifestyles. Rather than forsake one for the other, they believed in a little compromise here and a little conformity there. They were the philosophers of their time who wondered why the Romans should have everything. So they believed "When in Rome, do as the Romans do." Jesus rebuked them for being in error. He told them they knew neither the Scriptures nor the power of God (Matt 22:29).

The times we live in have produced a new generation of Sadducees, whom we could call "Happisees". They are the new Epicureans, for whom pleasure is everything. Like the Sadducees of old, they follow the maxim, "heaven helps those who help themselves". These are committed to perpetual celebration in and out of church and the acquisition of all that will make life here as comfortable as possible. They therefore seek escape from every form of hardship, pain or suffering. These have embraced a new gospel that suggests that if you are a Christian, you are to be free from sorrows, pain, failure or sickness.

It is therefore not difficult to see why the words of Jesus are so discomforting to them. Why should Jesus ever say, "Blessed are they that mourn" or "Happy are the sad" when it is much more popular to say, "Happy are those that never mourn?" This is why the way of the cross has for so long been offensive to many.

The most popular gospels of the day have little regard for the cross of Christ or its demands. They pay more attention to the dictates of Hollywood and celebrity culture. This culture thrives in the glamour of red carpets, celebrities, halls of fame and all that is considered politically correct. In the make-believe world of fashion, make-up, fantasies and escapes from reality fuelled by glossy media attention, those who do not pursue the same values are considered subhuman or miserable. The lure is so attractive that some want the best of both worlds. They pay lip service to Jesus and life service to celebrity culture. Such people want to follow Jesus, but not through the dusty paths of real life. They would rather identify with Jesus when it is convenient, but the rest of the time they identify with celebrities whose masks of deceit suggest that the rich and famous are immune from the realities of stress and pain that the underprivileged deal with daily. In the red carpet world of celebrity culture, the idea of the cross of Christ is too distant to be taken seriously.

The Gospel of the Cross

Today we must choose between the old gospel of the cross and this imitation gospel that denies the power of God. We need a fresh look at kingdom values rooted in the experience of Gethsemane and Calvary. The cross is the only stable point on which to stand. And the cross we embrace must remain the same old cross, not some modern invention. We must heed A. W. Tozer's words:

> The old cross slew men; the new cross entertains them. The old cross condemned; the new cross amuses. The old cross destroyed confidence in the flesh; the new cross encourages it. The old cross brought tears and blood; the new cross brings laughter. The flesh, smiling and confident, preaches and sings about the cross; before that cross it bows and toward that cross it points with carefully staged histrionics – but upon that cross

it will not die, and the reproach of that cross it stubbornly refuses to bear.⁵

What did this mean then and what should it mean to us today? The call of Jesus in Mark 8:34–38 gives us the answer. Jesus states clearly that:

> Whoever wants to be my disciple must deny themselves and take up their cross and follow me. For whoever wants to save their life will lose it, but whoever loses their life for me and for the gospel will save it. What good is it for you to gain the whole world, yet forfeit your soul? Or what can you give in exchange for your soul? If any of you are ashamed of me and my words in this adulterous and sinful generation, the Son of Man will be ashamed of you when he comes in his Father's glory with the holy angels.

Jesus makes a three-fold call: (i) to deny oneself, (ii) take up the cross and (iii) follow him.

The call of Jesus, "Follow Me", demands complete personal allegiance to him. Those who respond are expected to learn from him and identify themselves fully with him and his cause. This had serious implications then and should still have serious implications for us today.

There cannot be any following without forsaking. In the days of Jesus, for some, it was literal abandonment of home and work. Simon and Andrew left their nets and followed him; James and John left all and followed him; Matthew the tax collector and others did the same. Today his words have *not* changed and still ring true: "Those of you who do not give up everything you have cannot be my disciple" (Luke 14:33). For some, to follow him may mean forsaking jobs or preferred careers. For others, this may not be necessary – *but* all of us must surrender to his will and control. There will be some forsaking that cannot be separated from the call to follow him.

First of all, there must be a renunciation of *sin*. The call to follow Jesus is synonymous with the call to repentance. John the Baptist announced Jesus' coming by preaching, "Repent, for the kingdom of heaven has come near" and called on his audience to "produce fruit in keeping with repentance" (Matt 3:2, 8). When he came, Jesus also proclaimed, "Repent, for the kingdom of heaven has come near"

(Matt 4:17). Repenting means renouncing and turning away from the thoughts, words, deeds and lifestyles that are displeasing to God. Preachers of the gospel cannot shy away from speaking against sin and urging people to repent. It may sound offensive or embarrassing, but there is no other way. Confession of sin is a necessary condition for receiving God's forgiveness.

Jesus used very strong words in describing what repentance entails:

> If your right eye causes you to stumble, gouge it out and throw it away. It is better for you to lose one part of your body than for your whole body to be thrown into hell. And if your right hand causes you to stumble, cut it off and throw it away. It is better for you to lose one part of your body than for your whole body to go into hell. (Matt 5:29–30)

These words are not to be taken for granted. Sin must be renounced. Renunciation leads to restitution.

Secondly, there must be a renunciation of self. We have just read Mark 8:34–35, which says that whoever wants to be Jesus' disciple must "deny themselves and take up their cross and follow me".

Denial of self is different from denying oneself things such as food, wealth and so on. True, we may sometimes have to deny ourselves things. Levi left all to follow Jesus (Luke 5:27–28). But much more important is that denial of one's self means being fully surrendered to Jesus. It means putting the "self", "me" or "I" to death so that Christ can truly be Lord and have pre-eminence in my life. My personal desires, will and control must submit to the Lordship of Christ. Only in this way can he be Lord of my life.

This was the call of our predecessors when they admonished those who came to Christ to die to "self". All self-will, self-centred desires and control must die for Christ to be Lord. We need to rediscover what it means to say, "not 'I' or 'me' but Christ". Like Paul, we must learn to die daily to "self" (1 Cor 15:31) because "self" symbolises human authority and control – "I am what I am", or "I own my own life so I can do what I please with it". No – you don't! Psalm 24:1 says "The earth is the Lord's, and everything in it, the world, and all who live in it;" Do you feel or say, "I am independent or autonomous"? No, you are not! You are responsible to God!

"Self" also symbolises human pride. The greatest sin is to elevate oneself more highly than God intends. The Scriptures teach clearly that "God opposes the proud but shows favour to the humble and oppressed" (Jas 4:6). People who have elevated themselves have suffered the consequences. In Daniel 4, we are told of how proud King Nebuchadnezzar was turned into a beast and made to eat grass before he came to his senses and realised that God is the Most High who lives forever:

> His [God's] dominion is an eternal dominion; his kingdom endures from generation to generation. All the peoples of the earth are regarded as nothing. He does as he pleases with the powers of heaven and the peoples of the earth. No one can hold back his hand or say to him: "What have you done?" (Dan 4:34–35)

Herod was another ruler who exalted himself more highly than he ought. When he arrogated to himself the worship that was due only to God, "an angel of the Lord struck him down, and he was eaten by worms and died" (Acts 12:21–22). God does not have to do that over and over again to put us in our right place, but it remains true that self steals God's glory and honour. It has the tendency to allocate to human beings what belongs only to God.

Self is in rebellion against God and always desires things that are contrary to his will. This is why it has no place in the gospel of the cross. Self-exaltation is the root of all spiritual failure. We often blame the devil or evil powers and principalities for our shortcomings when they succeed because self allows them to do so. Too many people go in pursuit of deliverance when what they need most is repentance.

We used to use the image that self sits on a stolen throne in the life of an unsaved person. It needs to be dethroned. It must die to make room for *Christ*, who must have pre-eminence in all things. Even when it manifests itself in Christian service or testimonies (which are at times self-advertisement), self must be dethroned. Self must be denied! Self must be sentenced to death for Christ to be truly Lord. Paul says, "I no longer live, but Christ lives in me" (Gal 2:20); David says, "not my will" (2 Sam 15:26) and John the Baptist says, "He must become greater; I must become less" (John 3:30).

To follow Jesus or be a Christian is to deliberately choose the cross of Christ. As Tozer says:

> The cross of old Roman times knew no compromise; it never made concessions. It won all its arguments by killing its opponent and silencing him for good. It spared not Christ, but slew Him the same as the rest. He was alive when they hung Him on that cross and completely dead when they took Him down six hours later. That was the cross the first time it appeared in Christian history.[6]

The cross and all it stands for remain as radical and revolutionary as ever. It still has no room for compromise, concession or compassion. It remains a symbol of shame, suffering and sacrifice. It means Christians are not called to a life of ease. Following Jesus can lead to suffering, persecution and even loss of life. That is why the New Age gospel of health and wealth is not and cannot be a gospel of the cross. Its pursuit of earthly convenience is contradictory to what the cross of Christ stands for.

But beyond the pain of the cross, new life is born. The cross of Christ transforms and refines. There may have been pain and tears, but there is also newness and purity of life. Those who have embraced this cross have never remained the same. They have become brand-new people (2 Cor 5:17; 1 Pet 2:9).

It is our stand on the cross of Christ that determines the difference between a saved person and one who has not encountered Christ in a personal relationship. When there is no room for the cross of Christ in the gospel we profess, there can be no real transformation. Tozer hit the nail on the head when he said:

> In every Christian's heart there is a cross and a throne, and the Christian is on the throne till he puts himself on the cross; if he refuses the cross he remains on the throne. Perhaps this is at the bottom of the backsliding and worldliness among gospel believers today. We want to be saved but we insist that Christ do all the dying. No cross for us, no dethronement, no dying. We remain king within the little kingdom of Mansoul and wear our tinsel crown with all the pride of a Caesar; but we doom ourselves to shadows and weakness and spiritual sterility.[7]

Ancient words, yet still so true! But do we believe it? Do we practise it? In place of this, we have become lovers of pleasures more than lovers of God. The gospel of champagne has called us to a life of ease and who can resist it? The paths walked by men like John the Baptist, Peter, John, Andrew and Paul have become so inconvenient for us. Many Christians would do anything to save their necks or have a good life. But the words of Jesus remain the yardstick, that "whoever wants to save their life will lose it, but whoever loses their life for me and for the gospel will save it" (Mark 8:35).

I have heard of a Russian brother who was imprisoned for his convictions about Jesus. Having tried various ways to make him renounce Christ, his torturers resorted to chopping off his fingers. Each time he refused to renounce Christ, a finger was chopped off. This continued until he had lost most of his fingers. Then some visitors had the opportunity to ask him what prayer request he had. He did not request to be freed from his suffering but requested prayer to be more like Jesus.

The person on the cross faces only one direction. "No turning back, no looking back and no going back." No more self-centred plans. Christ becomes all in all.

Following Jesus means that he is supreme in our lives; it means having supreme love for him and being committed to obeying him in all circumstances. It is to honour him above all else and let his "yes" be our "yes" and his "no" our "no". He comes before and above all else – family, friends or colleagues. He comes before society or public opinion. He comes before material things. Like Paul, the follower must be able to say, "For me to live is Christ and to die is gain." It is to be committed to Jesus consistently and continuously. It is only when there is this wholehearted followership of the master that a disciple finds rest. Dietrich Bonheoffer in *The Cost of Discipleship* has captured this well:

> Only the man who follows the command of Christ single-mindedly, and unresistingly lets his yoke rest upon him, finds his burden easy, and under its gentle pressure receives the power to persevere in the right way. The command of Jesus is hard, unutterably hard, for those who try to resist it. But for those who willingly submit, the yoke is easy and the burden is light.[8]

This gospel of the cross may not be popular to preach today because it always upsets the status quo. It demands that students who follow Jesus no longer cheat in exams; that husbands no longer cheat on their wives, that politicians no longer make false promises; that market women no longer hide rotten tomatoes under fresh ones to make a good impression; that businessmen no longer cut corners to cheat their customers; that leaders no longer steal from the national bank; and that "everyone who confesses the name of the Lord must turn away from wickedness" (2 Tim 2:19).

It may be politically incorrect or out of tune with contemporary values, but we must never compromise the truth. Jesus never compromised the truth for favourable results. He placed truth above positive responses to his message. Consider that the rich young ruler went away from Jesus *sad* (Mark 10:17–31). Today, it is so easy to tell someone in the shoes of that young man, "Hey, it's not that bad; I didn't mean to offend you. We can always work something out." How often we compromise truth to win big numbers or swell the offering. Yet today, Jesus still calls those who will follow him to, "Deny [themselves], take up the cross and follow him."

4

CHARISMATIC RENEWAL AND CONFUSION

There is no need for us to wait, as the one hundred and twenty had to wait, for the Spirit to come. For the Holy Spirit did come on the day of Pentecost, and has never left the church. Our responsibility is to humble ourselves before his sovereign authority, to determine not to quench him, but to allow him his freedom. For then our churches will again manifest those marks of the Spirit's presence, which many young people are specially looking for, namely biblical teaching, loving fellowship, living worship, and an ongoing, outgoing evangelism.

— John Stott

Something wonderful happened in the 1970s in secondary schools and university and college campuses in Nigeria (my home country) and around Africa. Spontaneous revivals broke out in fellowship groups. Fellowship meetings became longer and were characterised by tearful confessions, open repentance and reconciliation. Intercessory prayers focused on the unsaved. Bible study and teachings emphasised the need to turn away from sin and every appearance of evil. "Without holiness, no one shall see the Lord" was a common emphasis. Worship became more lively and focused on the holiness of God. There was a definite outpouring of the Holy Spirit on many students. In many meetings, his presence was felt most solemnly; there were moments of silence during prayers, groans of repentance that gradually broke into praise. Soft, silent praise often eventually lead to loud prayers in the Spirit, accompanied by speaking in tongues. Yet there was a sense of order. Such was the birth and growth of the charismatic renewal across Africa.

From Lagos, Nigeria, to Lubumbashi, DR Congo, and from Cape Coast, Ghana, to Cape Town, South Africa, fresh winds of renewal were blowing. From Nairobi to the coast, churches with deep roots in the conservative evangelical tradition were renewed with the fervour of the gospel as they became open to what was considered a new movement of the Holy Spirit. Their worship was renewed with the exercise of spiritual gifts. Not only did the spreading of the renewal significantly change the character of these churches in terms of their worship and the content of their teaching, it gave birth to new indigenous churches. Unfortunately, many of these churches have been deluded by the strange gospel, and some of their preachers trace their heritage to this great charismatic awakening.

Charismatic Renewal

The marks of the charismatic renewal of the 1970s were the emphasis on the Holy Spirit, the experience and exercise of spiritual gifts, devotion to prayer, and renewed evangelistic zeal.

The content of teaching revealed a new emphasis. The primary emphasis was on the role of the Holy Spirit and the necessity of experiencing the baptism of the Holy Spirit. This was expected to be validated by speaking in tongues. Songs emphasised the experience of the Holy Spirit's presence:

> The Holy Ghost fire (power) is coming down like a magnet (2x)
> The Holy Ghost fire (power) is coming down like a magnet
> Coming here, coming there, just like the days of Pentecost
> The Holy Ghost fire (power) is coming down like a magnet …

> All over the world the Spirit is moving
> All over the world like the prophets said it would be
> All over the world like a mighty revelation
> With the glory of the Lord as the waters cover the sea.

> I will fill your cup today to overflowing
> As the prophets did foretell
> Bring your vessels not a few
> I will fill your cup today to overflowing
> With the Holy Ghost and fire.
>
> I've found a new life
> I've found a new life
> If anyone asks me what's the matter with you my friend
> I'll tell him – I'm saved, satisfied, Holy Ghost-filled, tongue-speaking, water-baptised, demon-casting.
> I've found a new life
> Praise the Lord, hallelujah! Amen.

Equally stressed were the gifts of tongues and prophecy, which were commonly practised during meetings. Prophecies could occur at any time during corporate prayer and, while others remained quiet, the person with the prophecy spoke aloud. The content of prophecy was always a word believed to have been given by God.

The reality of the supernatural world being responsible for natural events was a common teaching. Spirits and demons were held responsible for some of these and they were to be bound or cast out. Fasting and prayer were encouraged at all times. There was a strong awareness of signs and wonders as the work of God, which is possible today as against the emphasis on reason, the need for faith. Miracles were emphasised, including healing for the sick and the raising of the dead. I can recall vividly how strong this emphasis was. I can recall some situations where some students died of natural causes and their colleagues rejected it as the work of the devil. Special all-night prayer meetings were held in an attempt to raise the dead. In most cases, the dead remained dead!

The theme of restoration, renewal, revival or divine intervention in human affairs became very common. Other popular emphases were the power of faith and the working of miracles. Divine healing was also stressed and it was common for some students to abstain from all medication. There was also a focus on the impending end of the world, with much teaching about the Rapture. The emphasis on the Rapture in the seventies was matched with an orientation toward frugality. Many students believed that it was wrong to keep a bank account because of the imminent return of Christ. Equally emphasised was the reality of the supernatural world being directly responsible for natural events. Special deliverance sessions were organised for deliverance from the powers of evil spirits. Fasting and prayer conferences began to take place regularly.

There was more commitment to private and public prayer. Rather than a prayer being said by an individual with others responding with "Amen" at the end, everybody prayed aloud at the same time, and spontaneously. Prayer meetings became much longer, often going on for two to three hours. There were also all-night prayer meetings, beginning at about 10 P.M. and continuing till dawn. It was common to hear students praying aloud and in tongues in various hostel blocks very early in the morning.

Worship sessions were also characterised by choruses and hand-clapping, interspersed with testimonies and accompanied by dancing. Activities during meetings included much use of hand gestures, jumping and occasional running around during praise and prayer sessions. Hand-clapping, which had been discouraged by earlier evangelical missionaries, became the norm, and ecstatic utterances brought a new dynamism to meetings.

I experienced this when I was a student at Ahmadu Bello University in Zaria, Nigeria, between 1974 and 1976. I also witnessed it on other campuses. Not only did our meetings change, but so did our lives. There was a sense of purity. Fellowship was honest and transparent. One could almost feel the truthfulness, the lack of any form of deceit, the transparency in relationships, the sobriety and the love. The emphasis on restitution resulted in several stolen books being returned to their owners or to libraries. There was freshness about this renewal. Things were really different, and so we sang, "Things are different now, something happened to me, when I gave my life to Jesus."

One of the clearest fruits of this renewal was the evangelistic zeal of students. We were convinced (and still are) that the primary purpose of the baptism of the Holy Spirit is to give us power to evangelise. Spiritual gifts are believed to be for the same purpose. This clearly motivated students to go out to share the gospel. It became popular among Nigerian Fellowship of Evangelical Student (NIFES) groups to talk of aggressive evangelism, which meant boldly presenting the gospel to individuals or groups of people. Some students abandoned school to take up complete engagement with evangelisation. A sense of urgency was created by the emphasis on the imminent return of Christ that came with the charismatic renewal.

Many of us thought we were the first to have experienced the Holy Spirit and his ministry so powerfully. We heard rumours of similar events in other parts of the world, but knew very little of our historical antecedents in the revivals in the late 19th and early 20th centuries.[1] Key among these were the events at Bethel Bible School in Topeka, Kansas, where on 1 January 1901 students spoke in tongues under the tutelage of Charles Fox Parham. This was followed shortly by the Azusa Street Revival, which began when a black holiness preacher from Houston, Texas, by the name of William Seymour, felt led by the Holy Spirit to go to Los Angeles to preach the gospel. He was said to be a man of small stature and blind in one eye. As he preached, the power of the Holy Spirit came down on the audience, people spoke in tongues and there were reports of other miracles. The event was initially dismissed because he was a black American, but later whites joined him and the revival spread to other places. There was free mixing of whites and blacks, Mexicans and Asians at a time when racial lines were quite significant.[2] New Testament and select Old Testament passages like Joel 2 were used, with a lot of emphasis on prayer and prophecy. Other emphases included initial conversion and the baptism of the Holy Spirit as a second experience accompanied by tongues. The Holy Spirit was believed to be very much present as blacks and white worshipped and prayed into the night. The Azusa Street Revival lasted three full years. Christians from all over North America, Europe and other parts of the world began to visit Azusa, and from there carried the fire of revival home. From there the flames spread to places like England, Finland, Africa, Russia, India and Latin America (not necessarily in that order).

Transition and Change in the Charismatic Movement

In Africa the charismatic renewal rapidly expanded the content of its teaching and shifts in emphasis diversified its identity. While in Nigeria and other parts of West Africa it began as a separatist movement, it gradually became more accommodating and by the 1980s was embraced by many mainline denominations. However, trends of accommodation of worldliness also emerged in the 1980s and contributed to the proliferation of prosperity preachers in the 1990s.

As we have observed, in most parts of Africa where this renewal movement broke out in the 1970s, in addition to the emphasis on the role of the Holy Spirit in the believers' life, there was strong emphasis on the necessity of repentance as the first step to salvation. There was an emphasis on the need for assurance of salvation and restitution for things done or of things stolen before one became a Christian. Furthermore, there was strong emphasis on turning one's back on the world to live a life of holiness. Ethical morality was encouraged in all aspects of life. There was a commitment to personal vocal witnessing about the gospel to others and an emphasis on the cross of Christ and willingness to suffer for Christ if need be.

However, insufficient teaching and a loss of focus on the more fundamental aspects of the gospel led to a preoccupation with gifts and a definite shift away from the cross. Self-promotion crept in and people began to claim for themselves the glory that was due only to God. We began to attribute spiritual exploits and evangelistic results to our own faith, our own zeal and to our being filled with the power of God. The focus began to be more on humans than on God. The recipients of the gifts began to be more important than the giver. It became "my gift of tongues", "my ministry gifts", "my outreach", "my converts" and so on. We began to major in what promoted us. There was also a greater focus on the more visible gifts of the Holy Spirit such as public prophesy, preaching and tongues than on the disciplines of the faith or the fruit of the Spirit. The words pastor, evangelist, prophet, bishops and even teacher gradually shifted from being associated with a ministry role and became titles. "Upward mobility" resulted in increased numbers of self-appointed "apostles".

Suddenly, most prayer meetings began to turn into sessions of uncontrolled prophecy. A sister or brother would stand up, alter her or his voice, begin, "My children, My children", and say things that were not necessarily backed by Scripture. Others would say things that were in fact merely veiled quotations from Scripture rather than a specific "word of prophecy". Discerning hearts should have known that what was happening was more self-exhibition than a word from the Lord; however, such behaviour went unchecked. Speaking in tongues became the order of the day, with scarcely any interpretations. Meetings started becoming a battleground for competing voices in tongues and prophecy.

As for preaching, every new convert became a preacher and with the help of a piece of wood, or a piece of signboard plus a little paint, a new ministry or church was born. The tragedy is that at the same time there was a slipping back from the emphasis on character and conduct. It was okay to prophesy and continue in sin. By the mid-1980s the moderation that marked lifestyle and governed modesty in the 1970s began to fade. Churches became parade grounds for the latest fashion. It became okay to be worldly and Christian. Frugality and stewardship gave way to the delusions of prosperity and materialism. Sobriety gave way to arrogant pride. Noise overtook any form of meditation. The spirituality of noise replaced the spirituality of contemplation and silence in the presence of God. Christian identity became more fluid as spirituality kept being redefined. By the end of the decade, we had lost the simplicity of Christ.

Firstly, there was more emphasis on gifts than on the fruit of the Spirit. In the 1970s it was common to hear sermons on Galatians 5:22–26. But in the 1980s, stressed only the gifts of the Holy Spirit. In the Nigerian context this new trend of emphasis on gifts gave us a new breed of ministers who set themselves up as "presidents" and "founders" of ministries, even though some of them had questionable moral records and had little or no grounding in the Scriptures. There was an obsession with titles such as "Reverend" or "Reverend Doctor", "or Bishop", or even "Apostle". These titles were not necessarily backed up by any formal qualifications, but nevertheless their acquisition was celebrated in expensive ordination, installation, or coronation ceremonies.

When I investigated how some of these titles were obtained, I discovered a strong link with American televangelists. Whenever they visited Nigeria, Ghana, or some other African country, they would reward their faithful hosts with such titles. They would also organise short-term ordination training after which participants would be ordained as "Reverends" or "Bishops". This was a sharp departure from the 1970s when we were content to call one another brother or sister.

Secondly, the focus on people gave birth to splits and the proliferation of ministries and churches. In cities in Nigeria it is not uncommon to see a single building housing two or three churches. I have seen several three- or four-storey buildings with a different church on each level, each worshipping at much the same time on Sundays and each maintaining the same times for midweek programmes! The lives of members of many of these churches run clockwise round the church with back-to-back programmes from Sunday to Saturday. A pastor once told me the only way to avoid having his sheep lured to greener pastures is to keep them busy all week feeding them *his* grass! Talk of sheep stealing is common. This is inevitable because the patronisers of some of these churches are restless youths or urban yuppies in search of something new. They soon grow tired of being in the same spot and move on to where the latest miraculous attraction in town beckons.

Hence the proliferation of churches was not necessarily always a result of evangelistic efforts. It was often more of a reshuffling from one group or church to the other. The rate at which breakaway factions regrouped to start new churches and ministries became alarming. The trend went something like this:

SCENARIO 1: An individual or a group of people within a church see the need for more fervour and depth. In their own personal pilgrimage, they have experienced a deeper or closer relationship with God or, as is often the case, a new experience with the Holy Spirit. They want this new fervour or experience to spread through their church but find the leadership either too slow or unwilling to embrace their new discovery. Either because of insufficient dialogue and prayer or sheer impatience, the group breaks away, believing their aspirations are unattainable in their present context. So out they move with a new name reflecting their convictions. It could be New Generation Holy Ghost Assembly or something like End Time Battle-Axe of God Ministries. I know of a faction in Lagos that broke away from a branch of the Evangelical Church of West Africa (ECWA) to form the Evangelical Pentecostal Church (EPC). Another group broke away from that to form the Evangelical Power Church (another EPC!).

This trend was more common in the latter part of the seventies when the younger generation who had experienced a more exuberant expression of Christianity on campus – lively worship, teaching and various experiences in or of the Holy Spirit and aggressive evangelism – became discontented with the more conservative life of older churches.

Finding the pastors and leaders of their churches conservative and un-accommodating, some shifted base to more "open" churches. Others, who believed in "the new movement of God", went straight on to establish their own prayer group or house fellowship. These soon graduated into "international ministries" and subsequently churches.

SCENARIO 2: Some zealous individual feels the church leader is taking all the limelight and not giving room for the younger ones to grow. Such a leader preaches all the sermons, controls the budget and possibly makes his wife the financial director. With little room for advancing their own cause, the restless subordinates disagree with the leader and move on with their sympathisers to start something new.

SCENARIO 3: Sharp disagreement over doctrine, finances and other less significant personal matters such as who leads the choir, who makes an overseas trip, or who runs a crusade have also led to splits.

All these developments may seem trivial but they have serious implications. Is the church really growing? Are we impacting the society? Are we reaching the unsaved people with the gospel?

From Confusion to Delusion

By the beginning of the 1990s there was much going on that bore little resemblance to the early charismatic renewal. Some groups and churches moved on to newer and stranger teachings that are not consistent with the renewal. Although they may still identify themselves in some ways with the charismatic renewal, their teachings and practices contradict it. We need to be careful not to classify such groups as charismatic movements. Some have become syncretistic, mixing biblical truth with pagan practices. Others have tilted more towards the occult with deification of their leaders and other practices. The line between spirituality and spiritism became very thin in the 1990s. Today it can be hard to distinguish some churches from cults.

The loss of focus on the fundamentals in some of the charismatic churches and fellowships in the 1980s led to all kinds of delusions in the late 1980s and 1990s. One of these is an obsession with materialism. The theology of prosperity that emerged in several charismatic groups in the 1990s implies that wealth is a sign of God's favour and blessing.

The pursuit of wealth in a way that would have embarrassed Christians in the 1970s became the quest of the 1990s. Pastors and bishops now ride in the most expensive cars in town and own the most flamboyant buildings. I know two "presidents" and "founders" in Lagos who boast of owning aircraft for the purpose of evangelism! That may be, but what is at issue here is not the material things in themselves but the implication that such possessions are a measure of the leader's spiritual maturity, intimacy and favour with God.

Another delusion that has emerged is what I call the deification of the ministers. With the quest for upward mobility and the perks attached to titles and positions, some of those being led have begun to put their trust in the leaders and bishops. Hero worship has increased to the extent that some show little concern about stealing the glory that belongs to God alone. Final authority is believed to rest with the pastor as churches shift from *Sola Deo* or *Sola Scriptura* to *Sola Pastora*. The pastor or "man of God" has final authority on matters of faith and lifestyle, thereby breeding laziness in personal Bible study. In some churches, members are encouraged to pray in the name of their bishop. There have been other strange practices, like the provision of a chair for the Holy Spirit or the provision of four chairs – one each for God the Father, the Son, and the Holy Spirit and one for the bishop.

In addition to the deification of people, there is the deification of objects. Having forgotten the transcendence of God, those who have made their bellies their gods have begun to deify and exalt man-made objects above the creator. Magical status is given to things like the bishop's "mantle", "anointing oil", "robes", "handkerchiefs" and "battle axes" with which deluded men think they can arouse God to action. Members of some churches believe the lie that if they use "magical" elements of the communion wine, bread, handkerchiefs, or anointing oil, they will not die until they attain the age of seventy.

Many other strange beliefs and practices abound and make it difficult for us to differentiate between churches and cults. For example, in 1994, some students and staff of the Nigeria Fellowship of Evangelical Students (NIFES) carried out a village outreach to Oluku Junction – a village near Benin City in Nigeria. During the house to house evangelism, they were warned not to enter a particular house because that was where many "pastors" come to collect charms for signs and wonders.

David Oyedepo, founder of Winners Chapel, preaches a gospel of vengeance. He urges his followers to place curses on their enemies. According to him, "vengeance is one of the prominent ministries of the Holy Ghost this end-time ... We are right in the days of vengeance of our God. None of your enemies will survive."[3] These enemies are not just impersonal things or beings but people. Oyedepo's several books record "testimonies" of people who have cursed or threatened their perceived enemies. Oyedepo has since taken to the use of various objects as magical remedies for any sign of earthly inconvenience. From distortions about the ministry of the Holy Spirit to what he calls the mystery of feet washing, he has combined the use of Scripture with what amounts to the ancient practice of witch doctors to offer solutions to all of life's problems.

I was reliably informed by a family friend who had contact with a bishop of one of the fastest growing charismatic churches of some weird things that occurred during the building of their new cathedral. The foundation was laid with some raw eggs broken and mixed with other things. In some groups like the Zoe Ministry, barren women are stripped naked for prayers of deliverance. All kinds of bodily examination are done. At times, the leader anoints their whole body by rubbing them with olive oil for deliverance from barrenness.

The charismatic renewal that began as a work of the Holy Spirit to renew the church to impact the world with the gospel has been hijacked by those who have turned the grace of God into a licence for all kinds of practices and self-aggrandisement. While there are ministers who have maintained both their integrity and that of Scripture, others have compromised and exported their distorted gospel to the ends of the earth.

There is no better way to recover lost ground than rejecting all falsehood and returning to biblical truth. Let us heed Tozer's admonition:

> It is time for us to seek again the leadership of the Holy Ghost. Man's lordship has cost us too much. Man's intrusive will has introduced such a multiplicity of unspiritual ways and unscriptural activities as positively to threaten the life of the church.[4]

5

THE "MODERN" PREACHERS

> *In recent years, the church has had too many celebrities and not enough servants, too many people with plenty of medals but not scars. To look at their lives and listen to their messages, you would never know that the gospel was about a humble Jew who was poor, rejected, and crucified; nor would you ever suspect that He said, "Blessed are the poor, For yours is the kingdom of God" (Luke 6:20) or "But woe to you who are rich, for you have received your consolation" (Luke 6:24, ESV).*
>
> — Warren W. Wiersbe

At 9:30 A.M. on Sunday 26 May 1996 I was with Dr. Yusuf Turaki, former ECWA General Secretary, at the Lagos Airport Domestic Terminal waiting to board a flight to Jos. Were we really at a terminal? It felt more like a public car park or a marketplace. Our departure for Jos was to be 10:00, but at 9:15 we went out to the tarmac to be sure we did not get left behind. Sure enough, there were lots of other people ahead of us. There were as many as ten aircraft on the ground, and any of them could be ours.

Since there was no other way to know, we inquired. Someone directed us to an aircraft belonging to Kabo, a private carrier, and we stood in line for it. Ten minutes later I asked the person in front of me if we were in the right queue for Jos. He said, "No, this aircraft is boarding for Kaduna." He pointed us to another plane and we quietly joined the queue there. Again, no one was certain that this place was going to Jos. We stayed there anyway. While waiting, several people came to inquire whether this plane was going to other destinations. There were also men offering tickets for sale for those who really wanted to be sure of getting on the flight, for a "small" fee.

The scene reminded me of public car parks in Africa where touts and self-appointed middlemen hassle and confuse travellers. Dr. Turaki wondered aloud why the management could not put up simple signs to say where each aircraft was going. He also commented, "where there is darkness, prophets abound". The significance of his statement did not strike me until I looked round and discovered that there were several touts giving directions to intending travellers – for a little "thank you" fee. I was surprised that we actually had boarding passes that day, except that the boarding passes read "Hajj 1993". And this was 1996! Someone must have printed too many boarding passes for 1993.

An aircraft close to us bore the name "Kolhol". We had been being lobbied to board this "brand-new" airplane that would depart for Jos promptly at 9:00! At 9:50, passengers were still boarding. A close look at the aircraft revealed that it was the same plane that we had originally known as Harko, which had then been reborn as Harka, and was now Kolhol. This was its third "reincarnation" in an attempt to make a third-hand Russian plane conform to local safety requirements. It is anyone's guess if a leopard can change its spots.

Dr. Turaki's statement, "Where there is darkness, prophets abound" is an apt description of current trends in the church. In the 1970s when things were more orderly and predictable, prophets were fewer or unknown. Nobody needed a prophet then to predict when the school year would end. But in the Nigeria of the 1990s, they were a necessity to let troubled parents know whether their children would take three or eight years to complete their degree because the universities were constantly closing. In the 1970s and early 1980s when the Nigerian economy was stable and more beneficial for all, nobody needed prosperity prophets to get their money "multiplied". All one needed was a good investment outlet or a solid bank where the security of one's deposit and interests was guaranteed.

These days with failed banks, collapsed finance houses and a depression that is both emotional and economic, we need prosperity prophets to teach us how to multiply our money. Sure enough, the prophets and preachers get richer and fatter while the flock is kept happy with new slogans and gimmicks. Like touts in the public parking or at Lagos Airport, the prosperity merchants make predictions and direct people to the vehicles that are least likely to get them to their destinations. In their wild imaginations, anything is possible.

This trend is not limited to Lagos or Accra. I have seen it spread from Freetown to Banjul, from Kampala to Lusaka, from Nairobi to Dar es Salaam. Khartoum, however, is still rather too hot for any modern preacher of the "gospel according to the stomach" to pitch his tent.

Man of God or "God" of Man

The prosperity preachers are "men of God" and they insist you know it. The lengthy sing-song way they are introduced in churches and meetings reminds one of how television celebrities and boxing champions are introduced. The church has gradually caught up with the tradition of Hollywood award-winning ceremonies. What has become so popular in the USA is now common in Africa. We introduce our speakers as celebrities.

Many "men of God" are ushered into meetings with a loud ovation and musical crescendo that may outshine Christ's triumphant entry into Jerusalem. Besides announcing their lengthy titles – Rev. (Dr.) Bishop, Prophet or Apostle as the case may be, the audience is told of their latest adventures. "Brethren" begins the Master of Ceremonies. "It gives me the greatest pleasure and joy, for my humble self to be called upon to such an impossible task of introducing this great man of God. In fact, I wish I knew how to begin but permit me to just do it as simply as I can. Our speaker for tonight, the man God will use, according to his counsel before the foundation of the world, is a man who is so filled with the Holy Ghost that demons tremble in his presence. He has been mightily used of God to accomplish great exploits in this nation. Through his crusades thousands, in fact, I can say millions, have been saved, delivered and Holy Ghost baptised. More than that, God has used him in many distant countries and continents."

By this time the audience is already clapping rhythmically and the drums are rolling. But the MC is not done yet. "But for our time, I would have told you of his many exploits in the spiritual realm. Tonight, we are so privileged because he has just returned from God's own country, the United States of America, besides a stopover in Australia. Our prophet tonight is in fact so busy that even his own church hardly sees him so we are more than blessed. Tonight, you will be blessed by him as you have never been blessed before. He is none other than the Rev. Dr. Evangelist (Apostle) … …"

The audience is then urged to give a clap offering to the Lord even though it is more than obvious who it is really offered to. The god of a man comes forward and begins with more eloquent nonsense about himself. The audience is blessed with more assertions of his self-significance.

Even as a student, when I heard this sort of introduction I somehow knew something was wrong somewhere. I knew that at the end of the meeting, many people would remember more about the speaker than about his message or Jesus. Sometimes I knew that lies were being told. Some of those presented as global preachers had never even travelled beyond their local regions. As a student, I hoped it was a trend that would pass. But the same things go on today.

I am of course not suggesting that we should be ignorant of who our speakers are. That could be very dangerous. But we ought to be able to differentiate between an assembly of God's people and a circus. All that is needed is the speaker's name and some brief information about where they are from or what they do; all the other excesses that inflate the ego are unnecessary baggage.

What Wiersbe once said of some churches in the United States has become true in Africa:

> A subtle change took place; many churches almost ceased to be congregations to worship God and became audiences gathered to watch men. Believers who used to be participants in sacred liturgy became spectators at a religious performance. "Sanctuaries" dedicated to the worship of God became "auditoriums" where the goats laughed and the sheep languished. We began to worship what A.W. Tozer called "the great God entertainment".[1]

This trend has left us with so-called "men of God" who are full of themselves and bask in the illusion of grandeur. These "flamboyant pre-eminencies" preach themselves much more than they preach Christ crucified. They are utterly different from John the Baptist who said, "He must become greater; I must become less" (John 3:30) and from Paul who said, "For what we preach is not ourselves, but Jesus Christ as Lord, and ourselves as your servants for Jesus' sake" (2 Cor 4:5). The Apostle Paul never used his title as flamboyantly as today's pseudo-apostles do. He referred to himself as "Paul, a servant of Christ Jesus, called to be an apostle, and set apart for the gospel of God" (Rom 1:1). First and foremost, he calls himself a servant in the sense of a bondservant or slave. Paul knew what it meant to be a slave in the old Roman world. Slaves were another person's property with no legal rights of their own. They had to do what they were told and go where they were sent. They had to respect, obey, suffer or even die. That was how Paul saw himself in his relationship with Jesus Christ. But while slaves in the Roman world were bondservants against their will, Paul's commitment came from a willing heart. Note that he calls himself a servant of Jesus Christ before adding "called to be an apostle". For Paul, it wasn't the title that mattered; it was the service. He had a testimony of obedient service. Many of today's ministers would rather be apostles than slaves to the Lord.

We face a major crisis today. A number of people have told me how they go to church longing to encounter Jesus, and how disappointed they have been that Jesus has often been marginalised both by the "men of God" and everything else that transpires in church. Jesus and the proclamation of the gospel keep being squeezed into oblivion by "more important matters" – blessing the minister, celebrating a birthday, commemorating a car or building and multiple appeals for funds.

Many years ago, some Greeks went to Jerusalem to worship during a festival and approached Philip with a request: "Sir, they said, we would like to see Jesus" (John 12:21). Like them, many in our generation long to see Jesus! They have heard rumours about him; now they want to see him. Some have heard that Jesus is love. That he is the Lord of the universe and is full of grace, truth and compassion. They have heard that Jesus is "the way, the truth and the life". Many have also heard that he came into the world to save sinners, not to condemn them. They have heard so many other things about Jesus. Now their deepest longing is to see Jesus for themselves. They want to see his grace, truth, love and compassion in the flesh. Some have such pressing needs that, having lost faith in other people and systems, they long for Jesus. It is Jesus they really want to see in church, not the flamboyance of cathedrals, the glamour of the parking lot or the latest fashion in town. Not the lengthy introduction of ministers or power-brokers; just Jesus and his word to them. When such people truly encounter Jesus, they'll take the fragrance of his love and salvation into the weekdays and public arena.

The story is told of a certain church that had a beautiful stained-glass window just behind the pulpit. It depicted Jesus Christ on the cross. One Sunday there was a guest minister who was much smaller than the regular pastor. A little girl listened to the guest for a time, then turned to her mother and asked, "Where is the man who usually stands there so we can't see Jesus?" Sometimes Christians can become the obstacle preventing the world from seeing the real Jesus when what we are and how we live overshadow him. We can grow so big or so visible that Jesus the Lord of creation becomes the hidden factor. Jesus must be restored to his rightful position in the church he owns.

There is great need in the church today to rediscover the simplicity of Christ. Our Lord himself was obedient unto death before he was highly exalted. I once heard Tony Campolo preach a sermon in which he referred to titles and testimonies. He said Pharaoh had a title, but Moses had a testimony. Nebuchadnezzar had a title, but Daniel had a testimony. King Agrippa had a title, but Paul had a testimony. Yes, Pilate had a title, but our master Jesus has a testimony. It is the testimony that matters, not the title.

The Lure of the Crowd

The Lord did not succumb to the lure of the crowd. They were so impressed with him once that they tried to force him to become king, but he resisted their enticement.

It is easy to fall into the trap that Jesus avoided. Speaking about John the Baptist, Jesus said:

> To what can I compare this generation? They are like children sitting in the market places and calling out to others: "We played the pipe for you, and you did not dance; we sang a dirge, and you did not mourn." For John came neither eating

nor drinking, and they say, "He has a demon". The Son of Man came eating and drinking, and they say, 'Here is a glutton and a drunkard, a friend of tax collectors and sinners." But wisdom is proved right by her actions. (Matt 11:16–19)

Many have thrown wisdom into the wastebasket of popular opinion.

Christ did not commit himself to the crowd no matter how popular he was with them. He even questioned someone who called him "good". What our Lord was wary of, many of us are eager to relish. When we are called "good", we encourage people to call us "perfect". But it is only false prophets who enjoy universal favour. Jesus said, "Woe to you when everyone speaks well of you, for that is how their ancestors treated the false prophets." (Luke 6:26) The temptation that Jesus resisted, our modern-day preachers indulge in.

Paul said very clearly to the Thessalonians:

> We speak as those approved by God to be entrusted with the gospel. We are not trying to please people but God. (1 Thess 2:4)

To the Galatians he said:

> If I were still trying to please people, I would not be a servant of Christ. (Gal 1:10)

Paul was not moved by the human opinion or the feelings of the crowd. Again, Wiersbe is right when he says:

> Many ministers are governed today by popularity and not by integrity, by statistics and not by Scripture. A false prophet asks, "Is my message popular?" While the prophet of God asks, "Is my message true?" You can't please the crowd anyway, so why try? One day they want to play wedding and the next day they want to play funeral! One week they complain because the preacher is in his study too much, and the next week they scold him for making too many visits!"[2]

The Pursuit of Miracles

The overemphasis on the miraculous and spectacular among the "health and wealth" preachers has led to a general quest for an easy life devoid of some day-to-day realities. There seems to be an assumption that the more miracles people see, the more they will repent and turn to Jesus. It was clear that in the days of Jesus, miracles did not always make people repent or trust in him. The opposite was in fact true. The cities in which he performed the most miracles did not repent (Matt 11:20–24). They probably got too excited about the signs and forgot who performed them.

When miracles become the primary focus, it is very easy to pursue the signs and fail to see the Saviour. Encouraged by modern evangelists who preach miracles rather than Jesus Christ crucified, there are many who follow Jesus primarily for miracles and do not know of the love of God reaching out to save them from their sins. There are still many who are like the crowd in John 6, who followed Jesus because of the miracle of feeding the five thousand; they follow him primarily for signs and wonders today. That crowd was so impressed that they intended to make Jesus king by force. He was the kind of king they wanted; one that would ease the pains and inconveniences of life by miracles. But the miraculous feeding did not seem sufficient to make them believe in Jesus. Even after Jesus tried to make them focus on him, rather than on the miracle, they still asked him, "What sign then will you give that we may see it and believe you? What will you do?" (John 6:30)

Yet we remain committed to the "gospel" that emphasises signs and wonders and say little about human depravity and people's need for God's saving grace. We love the excitement that comes with teachings that stress the extraordinary and the supernatural but remain silent on the basic truths of the gospel. There is a problem with the gospel that sees God as a miracle worker but downplays the miracle of conversion and the new birth.

Absence of Integrity

These modern preachers affect their church members far more than they do society at large. They have a noisy presence but not a transforming one that can challenge or hinder the corruption of public or private life. Some people are attracted to their gatherings not so much because they want to see Christ but out of curiosity to see the spectacular style of the preachers. When they find that there is a contradiction between their message and their lifestyle, they soon drift off to more appealing things. While many operate in the name of Christ, they lack the presence and the character of Christ.

Fraudsters and Tricksters

Many so-called preachers are out to fleece the flock rather than feed them. I know of one who was a pastor with a prominent denomination. He got involved in an extramarital affair and was challenged by the leadership of his church. Rather than submit to correction, he abandoned his wife and children and eloped with his new love. She provided funding to buy a plot of land and to put up an elegant building that houses his new church, which is full to capacity and overflowing. He is a gifted speaker and none of his associates ever question his integrity. No one seems to be bothered that he abandoned his wife and picked another.

I know of someone who was a bank manager involved in all kinds of fraudulent practices. In a bid to discard his soiled testimony, he moved to Lagos. However, his nature followed him to Lagos where he continued in similar practices. Yet he started a church which he pastored and never lacked followers. He combined pastoral work with banking and other financial dealings. When his banks and finance houses failed and collapsed in Lagos, he went underground to escape the law.

What Must We Do?

Why must we as the body of Christ wink at trends like these in the name of tolerance? Why have we so misunderstood the meaning of "love covers over a multitude of sins" (1 Pet 4:8) that we have fellowship with wilful sinners who disguise themselves as "men of God"? The word of God gives us principles that help us to distinguish the true teachers from the false ones, and correct teaching from wrong teaching. The Bible admonishes us to examine both the teachers' lives and their teaching on the basis of the revealed will of God. The time has come to demonstrate tough love, the love that says, "I love you brother, but I am afraid you've got this wrong and you've got to repent of it."

Paul clearly told Timothy to have nothing to do with those who have "a form of godliness but deny its power" (2 Tim 3:5). Likewise we must have nothing to do with those who suppress the truths of God by their wickedness. We must not be carried away by their eloquent nonsense or flamboyance. Rather we must "guard what has been entrusted to our care" and "turn away from godless chatter", which has made some depart from the faith (1 Tim 6:20–21). We need to keep our heads at all times and not be swayed by the emotional appeals of preachers of a different gospel.

6

MISREADING THE SCRIPTURES

> *I know that after I leave, savage wolves will come in among you and will not spare the flock. Even from your own number some will arise and distort the truth in order to draw away disciples after them.*
>
> — Acts 20:29–30

Several years ago I was travelling in the USA with the Rev. Harris Poole, a long-term missionary friend. It was a long drive, and to keep the conversation going he asked me what I had read that morning in my quiet time. I immediately answered that the key verse was, "But seek ye first the kingdom of God, and all these things shall be added unto you" (Matt 6:33 KJV). He asked if that was all the verse said, and I replied affirmatively. He then asked me to quote it again and I did. Still, he asked if that was all that was in the verse. I wasn't quite sure so he asked if I had my Bible nearby. I pulled it out of my bag and turned to the passage. I read the verse again and discovered that I had omitted the words, "and his righteousness". My mind (and possibly my heart) had been more on "all these things" and so I had skipped over the words about righteousness. Daddy Poole then taught me that righteousness is much more important than what is added to us.

Today, we need to very careful about how we read passages in the Bible. We must be alert for what is omitted, whether accidentally as in my case or deliberately. We must also be alert to deliberate twisting of the word of God to make it say things that it is not saying. Jesus asked the scribes, "What is written in the law? ... How do you read it?" (Luke

10:26) The best tool in the hands of preachers of a different gospel is manipulation of the word of God. Through a private interpretation, a prophecy or a new revelation, the truths of the word of God can be distorted. It is easy to over-emphasise or de-emphasise the Word to suit our subjective purposes. Without careful study, it is possible to assume Scripture is saying what it is not saying.

The students I work with like to sing,

> Abraham's blessings are mine
> Abraham's blessings are mine
> I am blessed in the morning
> I am blessed in the evening
> Abraham's blessings are mine.

Many of them have material blessings in mind. Yet the focus of the blessings we have by being the offspring of Abraham has very little to do with wealth or material possessions (Gal 3:6–14).

Misinterpretation of the Bible

Very often passages or verses of the Bible are isolated and interpreted out of their literary context. Take a popular passage in charismatic prosperity circles, the King James Version translation of Isaiah 45:11:

> Thus saith the Lord, The Holy One of Israel, and his Maker,
> Ask me of things to come concerning my sons, and concerning
> the work of my hands command ye me.

This verse is often interpreted to mean that God can be commanded. We are told that when we pray, we can command God to do anything we desire. However, a close look at the textual context of the verse will indicate otherwise. A reading through the whole chapter gives a very different perspective from verse 11 looked at in isolation. Or better still, referring to other versions of the Bible will put the verse in context. The same verse in the New International Version reads:

> Thus is what the Lord says – the Holy One of Israel, and its Maker:

> "Concerning things to come, do you question me about my children, or give me orders about the work of my hands?"

This same verse in the Living Bible says:

> Jehovah, the Holy One of Israel, Israel's Creator, says: "What right have you to question what I do? Who are you to command me concerning the work of my hands?"

Those who interpret the verse out of its literary context and only from the King James Version fail to see the true meaning. This is probably why someone like Robert Tilton concludes:

> We make our own promises to do our part. Then we can tell God on the authority of His word what we would like Him to do. That's right! You can actually tell God what you would like His part in the covenant to be.[1]

Pastor John Praise of Dominion Chapel in Abuja, Nigeria, who refers to his headquarters as God's headquarters, once preached on, "Developing a posture of wealth mentality". Referring to Lazarus and the rich man, he asked, "Why was Lazarus in Abraham's bosom?" His answer was, "Lazarus had such a poor mentality of himself and a poverty mentality such that when he got to heaven the gold street made him afraid. He could not live alone in his own mansion, so Abraham had to bring him on his lap to give him orientation about wealth. To avoid that, we have to learn to rebuke the spirit of poverty and confess positively."

This interpretation of this passage of Scripture is very different from what the original writer intended. Abraham was one of the great ancestors of all Jews. To the average Jew, resting in Abraham's bosom was the highest possible bliss anyone could wish for.[2] So when Jesus says that Lazarus, a poor beggar, was carried "into Abraham's bosom" (Luke 16:22, KJV), he was saying that Lazarus was at Abraham's side in paradise or heaven.

Pastor Praise also said that when his members told him that he was developing a pot belly, he answered by quoting the King James Version translation of Proverbs 11:25, "Don't you know that the Bible said 'a generous man would be made fat?'" He added that because he was giving to people, God was giving to him and making his soul (stomach) fat.

He is not alone in reading into Scripture what is not there. David Oyedepo of Winners Chapel also uses Scripture to back his emphasis on material prosperity. In the introduction to his book *Covenant Wealth* he writes:

> It is important to know that God is interested in the comfort of His people. He is excited when they prosper. He is happy when they are comfortable ... wealth speaks of comfort. It speaks of fulfilment, and God desires your comfort above everything else.[3]

He then quotes another verse commonly used to back prosperity teaching, "I wish above all things that thou mayest prosper and be in health, even as thy soul prospereth" (3 John 2 KJV). Bishop Oyedepo's interpretation of this text is:

> There are many things, but He said, "above all, above everything else, this is my supreme will." Above every other will, He wants you to be comfortable and healthy. You must get that into your spirit, that it is not the idea of a preacher; neither is it a prosperity movement; but God's idea that you be comfortable. That is His idea; that is His intent; that is His purpose. He wants you to be comfortable.[4]

Jimmy Bakker, a famous prosperity teacher in the USA in the 1980s, once used the same verse of Scripture to preach the same message. He learnt his lesson the hard way when in 1987 he lost it all. His PTL and Heritage USA empire collapsed and he was jailed for fraud. In an interview with *Charisma* magazine soon after his time in jail, Bakker had this to say concerning prosperity and 3 John 2:

> God's Word doesn't say, "To those whom God loves, He gives new cars and new houses and an easy life." I often used 3 John 2, "Beloved, I wish above all things that you prosper and be in health, even as your soul prospers", as the basis for teaching this prosperity message. But as I began to read that verse in prison, and while I read the entire New Testament

over and over, I asked God, "How can John be saying here that above all he wants us to be rich?" Then I realized that I needed to study the word "prosper" more carefully. I sent away for Greek and Hebrew Study Bibles, and I began to look up all the words in 3 John 2. I learned that what John was saying was a greeting. He was simply saying, "I want you to have a good journey through life, even as your soul has a good journey to heaven." This verse has nothing to do with money![5]

Jimmy Bakker also had the following to say about his previous method of Bible study:

During my days at PTL I used a method called "proof-texting" when I preached. I just picked verses out of the Bible that dealt with the same topic. But when I was in prison I studied the Scriptures in context. And I realized that many of my pet verses were taken out of context and had nothing to do with what I was using them for. You can make the Bible say anything you want. I used to take Luke 6:38, "Give and it will be given to you: pressed down shaken together, running over...," and I used it as a great verse about giving. But Jesus wasn't talking about money in that passage. He was talking about forgiveness. He was saying that the same measure you give out forgiveness will determine the measure you receive forgiveness.[6]

If Jimmy Bakker has repented of twisting Scripture, many others have not. Their manipulation of Scripture has produced all kinds of false teaching. One such is the deification of human beings by the teaching that Christians are little gods.

We Are "Little Gods"?

The Lord Jesus Christ was once asked what the most important commandment was. He referred the teacher of the law who asked the question to the commandment that God gave Israel through Moses:

> Hear O Israel, the Lord our God, the Lord is one. Love the Lord your God with all your heart and with all your soul, and with all your mind and with all your strength. (Mark 12:29–30; quoting Deut 6.4)

Thereafter he quoted a second commandment related to loving our neighbours as ourselves.

"Hear O Israel, the Lord our God, the Lord is one" is the foundation for Israel's monotheistic view of God. This is backed by several Scripture passages. In Isaiah 45:5 the Lord says, "I am the Lord, and there is no other; apart from me there is no God." Isaiah 45:6 and 45:22 re-echo the same point.

If Israel was faithful to that understanding of God, contemporary trends indicate that things have changed. There are now teachers within the church who claim that people are little gods. These include the likes of Earl Paulk, John Avanzini, Morris Cerullo, Kenneth Copeland and Charles Capps, to name just a few.

Earl Paulk claims:

> Adam and Eve were placed in the world as the seed and expression of God. Just as dogs have puppies and cats have kittens, so God has little gods. But we have trouble comprehending this truth. Until we comprehend that we are little gods, we cannot manifest the Kingdom of God.[7]

If we have trouble comprehending Paulk's truth, John Avanzini did not. He claims that the Spirit of God, "declared in the earth today what the eternal purpose of God has been through the ages ... that He is duplicating Himself on the earth."[8]

Avanzini's very close partner in ministry, Morris Cerullo, is as convinced as Avanzini that God's purpose is to reproduce himself. He had this to say:

> Did you know that from the beginning of time the whole purpose of God was to reproduce Himself? Who are you? Come on, *who are you*? Come on, say it: "Sons of God!" Come on, say it! ... And as we stand up here, brother, you are not looking at Morris Cerullo, you are looking at God. You are looking at Jesus.[9]

Another famous televangelist, Casey Treat, buys this theology of being Jesus and God. Preaching on Genesis 1:26, Treat once said to the crowd in his 3500-capacity auditorium at the Christian Faith Center in Seattle, Washington:

> The Father, the Son and the Holy Ghost had a little conference and they said, "Let us make man an exact duplicate of us." Oh, I don't know about you, but that does turn my crank!
> An exact duplicate of God! Say it out loud, "I'm an exact duplicate of God! [The congregation repeats it a bit tentatively and uncertainly.]
> Come on, say it. [He leads them in unison.] "I'm an exact duplicate of God!" "I'm an exact duplicate of God!" [The congregation is getting into it, louder and bolder and with more enthusiasm each time they repeat it.]
> Say it like you mean it! [He's yelling now.] "I'm an exact duplicate of God!" Yell it out loud! Shout it! [They follow as he leads.] "I'm an exact duplicate of God! I'm an exact duplicate of God"!" [Repeatedly] ...
> When God looks in the mirror, He sees me! When I look in the mirror, I see God! Oh, hallelujah!
> You know, sometimes people say to me, when they're mad and want to put me down ... "You just think you're a little god!" Thank you! Hallelujah! You got that right! "Who do you think you are, Jesus?" Yep!
> Are you listening to me? Are your kids running around here acting like gods? Why not? God told me to! ... Since I'm an exact duplicate of God, I'm going to act like God![10]

If there is any one televangelist who has promoted this teaching more than others, it is Kenneth Copeland. He claims:

> Every man who has been born again is an incarnation and Christianity is a miracle. *The believer is as much an incarnation as was Jesus of Nazareth.*[11]

In so doing he puts the believer at par with Christ. He also once said to his audience:

You don't have a god in you, you are one.[12]

Paul Crouch is known to have taught the same. On a Trinity Broadcasting Network television programme, he said:

> Do you know what else has settled in tonight? This hue and cry and controversy that has been spawned by the devil to try to bring dissension within the body of Christ that we are gods. I am a little god. I have his name. I am one with him. I'm in covenant relation. I am a little god. Critics be gone.[13]

Others who have affirmed and taught the same include Kenneth Hagin, Charles Capps and Robert Tilton. How have they arrived at this position?

Most of them have based their teaching on their understanding and interpretation of John 10:34–35 and Psalm 82:6. They claim Jesus says plainly: "Is it not written in your law, 'I have said you are gods?' and 'the Scripture cannot be broken.'"

The question we must examine is, why did Jesus say those words? Shortly before he said them, Jesus laid claims to deity by saying, "I and the Father are one".

> The Jews picked up stones to stone him, but Jesus said to them, "I have shown you many good works from the Father. For which of these do you stone me?"
>
> "We are not stoning you for any good work," they replied, "but for blasphemy, because you, a mere man claim to be God." (John 10:30–33)

They were clearly offended because of their rooted conviction that the God of Israel was only one.

Why did Jesus respond by asking "Is it not written in your law, 'I have said you are gods'?" Was he teaching that people were gods? How can this be reconciled with Israel's "The Lord our God, the Lord is one"?

The answer lies in the context of the passage Jesus is quoting, which is Psalm 82:6. Who are the "gods" referred to in this passage? The whole psalm is a word of judgement on unjust rulers and judges. In the context of Jewish culture in Old Testament times, earthly rulers and especially judges were referred to as "gods" because they were God's representatives. That is whom the psalmist is referring to in Psalm 82:1 and 82:6, as well as in Psalm 58:1. Some versions of the Bible translate the word as "rulers" or judges.[14] As God's representatives on earth, they are also called "sons of the most high" (82:6). Nothing, however, suggests that they were divine. Their actions contradict that, and 82:7 declares that they "will die like mere mortals" and "fall like every other ruler". Psalm 58, too, condemns unjust "judges". So in John 10:34, the point Jesus is making is more or less, "If unjust judges are called 'gods' how is it blasphemy for me, the chosen one of God, to call himself the Son of God?"

Those who use this passage to teach that we are little gods are missing the point completely. Are we really "gods"? No! The text was not referring to us but to those judges in Israel who were faithful to what God called them to be. If human beings are gods, how come we are a little lower than the angels? (Heb 2:7). If we are gods, how come we are still subject to death? If we are already gods, why should we hope for another resurrection?

In *Christianity in Crisis*, Hank Hanegraaff has traced the roots of this deification of humanity. He mentions M. Scott Peck, a psychologist who is popular in New Age circles. In his book, *The Road Less Travelled*, Peck says, "God wants us to become Himself (or Herself or Itself). We are growing toward godhood. God is the goal of evolution."[15] Then Hanegraaff traces the roots to Maharishi Mahesh Yogi, of Transcendental Meditation fame, who proclaimed, "Be still and know that you are God."[16] What was once in the domain of Eastern religions became the pursuit of Westerners as well. In literature and television series like Shirley MacLaine's *Out on a Limb*, where MacLaine declares, "I am God!, I am God!", Westerners are now told how they can be gods. And in Africa where we have turned in large numbers to embrace the one true God, we are being deceived to return to pre-Christian times when our kings ruled as gods.

What the early church fathers would have condemned outright as heresy has found increasing acceptance among some contemporary Christians. But if we return to Genesis, we will find that it is the same old temptation that led to the fall of Adam and Eve that has slithered into the church.

The Scriptures are also being manipulated to proclaim a variety of other heretical doctrines. How should we respond to all these? Paul's charge to Timothy remains a relevant guide, "Have nothing to do with such people" (2 Tim 3:5). He then told Timothy,

> But as for you, continue in what you have learned and have become convinced of, because you know those from whom you learned it, and how from infancy, you have known the holy Scriptures, which are able to make you wise for salvation through faith in Christ Jesus. All Scripture is God-breathed and is useful for teaching, rebuking, correcting and training in righteousness, so that all God's people may be thoroughly equipped for every good work. (2 Tim 3:14–17)

It is to this Scripture we must return. We must not be content to accept just what "men of God" teach us but, like the Bereans (Acts 17:11), we must examine the Scriptures every day to see whether what we have been taught is true or not.

7
COUNTERFEIT FAITH

Faith never means gullibility. The man who believes everything is as far from God as the man who refuses to believe anything.
— A. W. Tozer

It was the week before the final exams for the academic year. The leaders of the Christian Union planned a special all-night prayer meeting for all who wanted to succeed in the final exams. Since many members of the Christian Union (CU) desired success, the prayer meeting was packed full. The all-night prayer meeting went very well with times of prayer interspersed with praise songs and testimonies. Students left the meeting claiming success and believing that they would be "heads" and not "tails" in the forth-coming exams on the basis of Deuteronomy 28:13.

Weeks after the final examination, many of them were shocked to find that they had failed. What happened? Did they not claim success in the all-night prayer meeting? Careful investigations soon revealed that quite a number of them had not been diligent with their studies. Many had been too busy with various CU meetings and outreaches to attend to their studies. Several had skipped lectures because they were too tired from long late-night meetings. Yet they believed that just because they prayed and asked God for success, they would pass their exams. They overlooked or had not taken seriously enough an important verse of Scripture that says, "Faith without works is dead" (Jas 2:26, KJV). They had not studied enough, yet they expected God to reward them with good grades because of their faith. But their faith or confidence in sweat-less victory did not save them from "F" grades.

A medical student on another of our campuses said that God had told him not to attend lectures or study, and yet he would pass the final exams. It took the campus staff worker and some other elders to make him understand that faith without works is dead.

These stories illustrate the popular belief in some circles that those who follow Jesus will enjoy sweat-less victories. There are still many students who want to be "heads and not tails" without hard work.

These stories are not just isolated incidents in Nigeria. They represent a faith movement that has traversed the entire world. There is much talk about faith these days by all kinds of teachers, many of whom have distorted the biblical meaning of faith. As we shall see, a common thread of emphasis runs through most of their teaching, which is characterised by themes and catch phrases like "the power of faith", "seed faith" and "possessing your possessions".

The expression of the faith movement in Nigeria and other parts of Africa has its roots in the American faith movement. We can trace a connection between Benson Idahosa in Nigeria, Duncan Williams in Ghana and many other faith teachers elsewhere in Africa and some American televangelists. The American Bible belt, with Tulsa Oklahoma as its Jerusalem, has significantly influenced what is taught in charismatic prosperity churches and ministries in most parts of Africa.

The different expressions of the "faith" gospel have to do with a variety of styles and personalities, but the heart is the same. So we will deal with them by examining the American roots first before we consider their expressions in Africa.

Faith in Faith

A prominent father of the faith movement, Kenneth Hagin, has stated:

> Did you ever stop to think of having faith in your own faith? Evidently God had faith in His faith because He spoke words of faith and they came to pass ... In other words, having faith in your word is having faith in your faith. That's what you've got to learn to do to get things from God: Have faith in your faith.[1]

For faith teachers, faith begins by having faith in one's faith. You must have faith in your faith to get things from God. Whereas Jesus says, "Have faith in God" (Mark 11:22), most faith teachers say, "Have faith in your faith!" The basis of having faith in faith is that God himself has faith in his faith. Kenneth Copeland and Charles Capps, both American televangelists, have also expressed the same belief. Copeland teaches that God is a faith being and humans are faith beings. Therefore we have faith to operate in the same way "that God operates"[2] because it is faith that "activates God".[3] Charles Capps declared, "Some think that God made the earth out of nothing, but He didn't. He made it out of something. The substance God used was faith."[4] In a very subtle way Hagin, Copeland and Capps have replaced God with faith, and encouraged their followers to have faith in faith.

According to many of these faith teachers, faith is the answer to sicknesses and disease. The conviction is that disease is not physical but spiritual. In response to our confession of faith, God is expected to heal all diseases. Even in the face of sickness or disability, one is urged to deny the reality of the symptoms and confess the reality of wholeness to bring healing into reality. Kenyon says it all:

> I know that I am healed because He said that I am healed and it makes no difference what the symptoms may be in the body. I laugh at them and in the Name of Jesus I command the author of the disease (Satan) to leave my body.[5]

Kenneth Copeland equally believes that creative visualisation and confession can heal a person:

> When you get to the place where you take the word of God and build an image on the inside of you of not having crippled legs and not having blind eyes, but when you close your eyes, you just see yourself leap out of that wheelchair, it will picture that in the Holy of Holies and you will come out of there. You will come out.[6]

Given such an understanding of what faith is, it is not surprising that many of the faith teachers believe that there is a faith formula that yields the greatest results.

The Faith Formula

In his book *How to Write Your Own Ticket with God* Kenneth Hagin outlined and popularised the four steps in the faith formula. They are: Step 1 – Say it; Step 2 – Do it; Step 3 – Receive it; and Step 4 – Tell it.[7] Hagin says that Jesus appeared to him and told him that "if anybody, anywhere, will take these four steps or put the four principles into operation, he will receive whatever he wants from Me or God the Father."[8] "For good measure", Hagin adds, "it includes what one wants financially."[9]

From this faith formula, several other faith teachers have developed others.

Faith as Positive Confession

The primary instrument to translate faith into reality, according to faith teachers, is the spoken word. By this, most of them mean positive or negative confession. There is power and life in whatever confession we make. The origin of this is actually Kenyon who says, "A spiritual law that few of us realise is that our confession rules us."[10] If we confess positively, whatever we desire will come to pass. By our confessions, we bring into reality the very things we desire. Some teachers like Charles Capps encourage us to first visualise and then speak into reality the things we desire. He illustrated this by saying:

> This is the key to understanding the virgin birth. God's word is full of faith and spirit power. God spoke it. God transmitted that image to Mary. She received the image inside of her ... The embryo that was in Mary's womb was nothing more than the word of God. She conceived the Word of God.[11]

In Capps' understanding of the incarnation, it is the Word that Mary conceived; in the same vein, faith is the conception of the word of God.

Marilyn Hickey, another of the American faith teachers, has also argued that when this conceived word goes forth, it is powerful. She urges her hearers:

What do you need? Start creating it. Start speaking about it. Start speaking it into being. Speak to your billfold. Say, "You big, thick billfold of money." Speak to your check book, say, "You check book, you have been so prosperous since I owned you. You're just jammed full of money."[12]

This leads to another central concept in their teaching – the force of faith.

The Force of Faith

Kenneth Copeland has stated that:

> Faith is a power force. It is a conductive force. It will move things. Faith will change the human body. It will change the human heart. Faith will change circumstances ... The force of faith is released by words. Faith-filled words put the law of the spirit of life into operation.[13]

Thus for Copeland, faith is actually a dynamic force that changes any circumstance. This explains why there is a great emphasis on positive confession. So, for example, positive confession is what will bring wealth.

Conversely, negative confessions are to be avoided. Many faith teachers have chided Job for bringing calamity on himself; it was a result of his negative confessions. Charles Capps says, Job was not "under the anointing" when he said, "The Lord gives and the Lord takes away".[14] According to him, "Job activated Satan by his fear when he said, "the thing which I greatly feared is come upon me" (Job 3:25). Active faith in the word brings God unto the scene. Fear brings Satan on the scene."[15] Kenneth Copeland says, "When are we all going to wake up and learn God didn't allow the devil to get on Job? Job allowed the devil to get on Job."[16]

Many African preachers have swallowed this teaching hook, line and sinker. David Oyedepo teaches that, "Faith becomes a creative force when it finds expression in words that are spoken. The faith of God will amount to nothing except it finds expression in words."[17] He was echoing the words of Kenneth Copeland in a different way. Copeland's way of putting it is, "God cannot do anything for you apart from faith," because "faith is God's source of power."[18]

In the same way Oyedepo teaches, "Friend, there is no place your mouth cannot take you to. When you talk mediocrity it will become your garment and when you talk lack, you will have it until you become lack yourself!"[19]

What Is Faith?

We need to acknowledge that there are testimonies of those who have received results on the basis of this type of faith. Many have been healed in this way. Yet we must deal with the reality of those who had faith and were not healed. Dan McConnell gives a detailed account of one of those who believed in all these formulae and still suffered loss:

> One of the many tragedies illustrating the potentially disastrous effects of the conception of healing in the Faith movement is that of Wesley Parker, whose story is told in his father Larry's chilling book, *We Let Our Son Die* (Harvest House, 1980). After Wesley had been prayed for by a Faith evangelist, Larry and his wife Lucky decided to withhold insulin from their diabetic son. When Wesley grew ill and went into diabetic coma, the Parkers decided (as they had been taught) that Satan was attempting to deceive them with false symptoms. They continued to confess Wesley's healing until his death in diabetic coma on August 23, 1973.
> Believing that God would raise Wesley from the dead, instead of a funeral, the Parkers conducted "a resurrection service". When no resurrection came, Larry dismissed from the service all those who did not have faith for the miracle. Amazingly, Larry Parker held to his belief in Wesley's resurrection for more than a full year after his death. The Parkers were convicted of child abuse and involuntary manslaughter and each was given a five-year, probated sentence. (The sentence could have been 25 years in a federal penitentiary.) Because of their exemplary lives both before and after the death of their son, and because the judge

considered the Parkers good people (just highly misled), the court eventually reversed both verdicts. Whereas Wesley Parker is one of the better-known victims of the doctrine of healing taught in the Faith movement, there are many others, whose stories are just as tragic, and whose deaths were just as senseless.[20]

The greater concern, however, is not that the technique does not always work but whether it is true, in other words, whether such teaching about faith is biblical. Although it is not possible to deal with all the issues here, I have tried to raise them and ask readers to examine the various teachings in the light of the Bible and decide whether they are biblical or not.

I should point out that a number of scholars have carefully investigated the roots of the faith movement.[21] One such is Dan McConnell, who has traced its roots to E. W. Kenyon, who authored most of the teachings on which the faith movement is based. Kenyon freely admitted to his close associates that "he drew upon cultic, metaphysical sources in the formulation of his teaching."[22] McConnell concluded that "Kenyon's Faith Movement is a syncretism of New Thought metaphysics and radical fundamentalism, it is, in fact a different gospel."[23]

Kenneth Hagin then "single-handedly took Kenyon's teachings and from them forged a movement."[24] While one cannot call all those who follow in the steps of Kenyon, Hagin, Copeland and the like cultic, there is still much going on in the movement that constitutes a different gospel.

Our greatest need today is to return to the Bible to rediscover the true meaning of faith. While Scripture says in Hebrews 11:6 that, "without faith it is impossible to please God", we must know that not all that is called faith today pleases God. We must not assume that God is pleased with misconceived faith – a "faith" that has drifted from the biblical definition of faith, or with manipulative faith – a "faith" that is promoted to a gullible crowd by magician-like preachers. Worse still is faith that has misplaced its focus on the object of biblical faith.

Hebrews 11:6 continues, "Anyone who comes to him must believe that he exists and that he rewards those who earnestly seek him." Biblical faith must point to God as its sole object. Apart from the sovereign God, there is no basis for faith.

But before focusing on God as the sole object of our faith, we must examine some current popular trends that are a threat to this focus.

Misconceived Faith

Most people know that faith has to do with belief or trust in somebody or something. This is precisely the beginning of various misconceptions about faith. Some have taken it to mean belief in just anything. As long as you believe in something and you are sincere, you have faith. Since the emphasis is on just "believing", the object of faith becomes secondary. So we have "men of faith" who believe in Buddha or in Guru Maharaj Ji or Brahman. Occultists also believe in something, as do Mormons. This kind of trend soon gets even the most sincere person believing in his imaginations, however wild they may be. This is partly why all kinds of people and some governments had faith in the magic year – A.D. 2000 – when supposedly, there would be better housing for all, free health for all, a balanced diet for all and total eradication of guinea worms and cockroaches. But biblical faith is not gullibility.

Gullibility is the attitude that "all things are possible because I believe all things are possible". Gullible faith makes me believe I will pass my exams because I believe I will pass my exams – even if I don't take time to study. It can suggest that an all-night prayer meeting the day before exams start is as good as consistent and disciplined study. Gullible faith claims all the promises in Scripture without taking into consideration the conditions attached to them. Gullible faith makes one think positive confessions are as good as real. Biblical faith, however, is much more than positive thinking or confessions, regardless of how sanctified we think our imaginations are. It is much more than "faith in faith" which makes faith an end in itself. Faith based on a wrong premise or falsehood is not biblical.

Manipulative Faith

Misconceptions about faith are often encouraged not by outsiders but by people within the church, who place more emphasis on their subjective experience than on the object of biblical faith. Some manipulate both

Scripture and people to suit their own ends. Rather than emphasising the need for a relationship with God through the Lord Jesus Christ, they emphasise the extraordinary outcomes that may result from such a relationship. So people are stirred up to have faith not in God but in his gifts. In Scripture people are urged to come and see or meet Jesus, as Andrew did to Simon Peter and Philip did to Nathanael (John 1:40–46) or as the woman at the well did to her fellow townspeople (John 4:29). Many evangelistic meetings or crusades today urge people to come and see miracles – not Jesus. So crowds come, not to encounter Jesus Christ but to see extraordinary events. Thank God, when miracles do happen, some do come to faith in Christ. But when miracles don't happen, the crowd is disappointed not only in the "man of God" but in God as well.

The object of biblical faith must be God and all that a relationship with him involves, and not just signs and wonders. But the worst manipulation is when the object of faith ends up being the "man of God" himself. Advertisements and publicity urge people to come and see not Jesus but "Evangelist X" or "Prophet So and So" "who will shake this city". They speak of "this mighty man of God, with direct access to the throne of grace, who has come to storm this city". Quite a lot of people will attend out of curiosity to behold the wonders to be done by this "man of God". If remarkable signs and wonders do happen, the effect is like a magician shouting "come and see what I can make objects do" or "come and see what I can make God do". It is not only people and their faith who are manipulated but God as well. Faith is that which pleases God and not just what satisfies the whims and caprices of some individual.

Misplaced Faith

Any faith that is placed solely in miracles is far from biblical faith; it is misplaced faith. Faith is misplaced when it focuses belief or trust in anything other than God or makes God less than he is. This can be the case even when the objects of faith are symbols of God's presence. For example, when the Israelites launched a battle against the Philistines in 1 Samuel 4, their faith was in the Ark of the Covenant, which symbolised God's presence. They were surprised that even when the Ark was brought to the battlefront the Philistines slaughtered 30,000 of them, in addition to the 4,000 who had fallen in the first battle. Why did this happen? The Israelites were taking some things for granted. They forgot that their God was holy and could not tolerate sin in the camp. They also sincerely mistook the presence of the Ark and their accompanying loud noise as sufficient for victory over their enemies and underestimated the relevance of their personal relationship with God.

Misunderstood Faith

Perhaps the greatest misunderstanding about faith is the assumption that God rewards those who diligently seek him by making life easy for them through extraordinary exploits. Faith is abused when we assume it is a magical force that makes virtually anything possible simply because we "believe". We sometimes think that those who suffer hardship or inconveniences lack faith. We think real people of faith overcome all difficulties and have sweat-less victories. But this whole notion contradicts biblical faith.

Those who teach this idea like to speak about the heroes of faith in Hebrews 11 who accomplished extraordinary things. But their reading of the text is often very selective. It is very easy to talk of the faith of Abel and of Enoch who "did not experience death." Then of Noah who was miraculously delivered from the flood and of Abraham for whom God provided an instant replacement for his son, Isaac, just before the latter was to be sacrificed. We then run quickly past Isaac and Jacob because nothing seems too dramatic about them. How many of us would like to work for seven years to earn our bride, as Jacob did, and discover we have the wrong woman, then wait and work for another seven years to eventually marry the love of our life? It is easier to talk of Sarah who gave birth even though she was over-age and barren.

In the exposition of Hebrews 11, we often skip verse 13 because it is not too convenient to talk of dying without receiving the things promised. So we go on through Joseph to Joshua before whom the walls of Jericho crumbled until we get to Rahab. Again there is a bit of unease about Rahab because she is not the typical kind of person to be associated with the kingdom of God. So Rahab is brushed aside for the "real" heroes of faith, especially as it is recorded in the King James Version.

I confess that this was how I read Hebrews when I was much younger. Those from whom I learnt about faith almost made me believe that Hebrews 11 ended with the 35th verse. There was usually complete silence on verses 36–37. The closest I came to hearing anyone teach on this was the apology that often comes after verse 35, "We would have gone on with the rest of this passage but for the shortage of time." You see, the rest of the chapter just doesn't seem to fit. I had come to believe that faith was about extraordinary or supernatural encounters. Faith was never to be sick or it was about refusing medication and receiving "divine" healing when sick. Hospitals were meant for those who lacked faith. Faith was about having the best grades in exams simply because of being a child of God. Faith was to reject any negative thing happening to me. It was to always have a testimony of something positive and extraordinary. So it was much more convenient to talk of heroes of faith who subdued kingdoms and shut the mouth of lions.

It later became clear why there wasn't much excitement about the rest of Hebrews 11. How could anyone talk of facing jeers and flogging or being chained and imprisoned when there is a verse that says, "If God is for us, who can be against us?" (Rom 8:31)" Why should anyone talk of being stoned, being sawed in two and being put to death by the sword when we serve a God who "is mighty in battle"? And why should it ever be written that, "These were all commended for their faith, yet none of them received what had been promised"? (v.39). It was this verse that eventually helped me to reread Hebrews 11 to discover that being a man of faith was not just about having "sweat-less" victories or having all things work out for me the way I confess them to be.

There is actually no indication that any of those giants of faith in Hebrews had an easy life. Not even those who stopped the mouths of lions. Was it faith without works that made Abel offer God a better sacrifice than Cain did? What was it like for Noah to build the ark while his neighbours and others jeered? What was it like for Abraham to pack his bags and move out of town simply because God told him to "even though he did not know where he was going"? What was it like to wander around in tents as he did? Was he comfortable when he took

Isaac up the mountain to be sacrificed without confiding in his wife, Sarah? Do we think he knew that God was going to provide a substitute for the sacrifice? What was it like for Moses to lead the kind of people he led and not be able to enter the Promised Land?

A careful reading of Hebrews will show that faith is not just about instant victories and sweat-free success. Most, if not all, of those listed faced risks to live as they did and accomplish what they did. They all had to have guts to have done all they did. The right word is perseverance or endurance. Rather than being certain of results because of using the right formula, true faith is about waiting, enduring, pressing on even when the end is not certain. It involves giving up all confessions and formulae and depending entirely on God. If we are to be true to biblical faith, we must dismiss the illusion that it is a magical wand that brings instant relief in all circumstances we may find ourselves in.

Grace (not her real name) grew up being taught that once someone follows Jesus, there will be no more sorrows or disappointments. She was made to believe that with God all things are possible. She fervently believed that if she walked closely with God all things would go well. And should anything go wrong, she could expect a miracle to fix it. She loved the Lord and enjoyed her Christian life. Most of her prayers were answered and she testified often of God's grace and sufficiency. Then her boyfriend left her for another girl. She did not understand why that should happen to her. She had held on to high hopes of their getting married. She could not accept that her boyfriend had left her. She believed he would come back. But he never did. He went off with the other girl. She was not only disappointed with her boyfriend but also with God for allowing that to happen to her. "If God loves me and really cares, why should He allow 'John' to leave me?" she asked. "Why should I serve God when he will allow such things to happen to me?"

Grace felt bitter towards God because the theology she was brought up with more or less says, "those who follow Jesus will have all that they want, when they want it and how they want it". God is there primarily to ensure that one is free from stress, heartache and earthly inconveniences. We must restate that the essence of faith is complete trust and dependence on God. What then does it mean for God to be the sole end of our faith?

Faith in God

When we ask, "faith in whom?" our response must be God and all that he stands for. It is not just about positive confessions. The foundation must be a personal and continuing relationship with God through Jesus Christ and every attending implication. "Anyone who comes to God must believe that he exists" (Heb 11:6) implies the necessity of a personal relationship with God as the beginning of faith. There must be personal trust and confidence in the totality of who God is. Faith must make us know God in all his greatness, power, righteousness, loving kindness, judgement, and so on. Such knowledge must in turn affect our lives in terms of what we are in relationship with God. That is why Christ came, so that having been made new creatures in Christ, we may have unhindered access to God.

The second part of Hebrews 11:6, "and that he rewards those who earnestly seek him" does not mean that God is just there to satisfy all our requests or demands. It implies that faith also involves belief and confidence in God's saving acts, however he may choose to fulfil them in our individual lives. It is a continuing personal attitude towards God and submission to his sovereign will. If he chooses to do some extraordinary things in our lives as part of his saving acts, so be it. Our faith and trust must remain steadfast. If he chooses not to do the extraordinary things that we expect, our faith in him must remain steadfast. Biblical faith does not abandon God because he has not done something for me. True faith is consistent confidence in God despite all that contradicts him. Faith is continuing with Jesus even when his sayings or words become too hard (John 6:60–67). Faith is looking to God, to Jesus, even when what we desire does not seem to materialise. It is not a one-time act but a continuous pursuit of God.

If God is the object of our faith, we must seek to please him by our obedience and lifestyle. When God first called Abram and asked him to go to a place he did not know, Scripture says he went out, not knowing where he was going (Heb 11:8). He simply obeyed God. Then in Genesis 17:1, God told Abram, "walk before me and be faithful". God wanted him to live a blameless life. This is his call today to those who will live by faith, with the ultimate goal of being like Jesus, of whom God said, "This is my Son, whom I love; with him I am well pleased" (Matt 3:17).

8

THE DELUSIONS OF PROSPERITY

The meaning of earthly existence lies, not as we have grown used to thinking, in prospering, but in the development of the soul.
— Alexander Solzhenitsyn

Jesus answered, "Very truly I tell you, you are looking for me, not because you saw the signs I performed but because you ate the loaves and had your fill. Do not work for food that spoils, but for food that endures to eternal life, which the Son of Man will give you. On him God the Father has placed his seal of approval."
— John 6:26–27

In chapter six of the Gospel according to John, we are told that "a great crowd of people" followed Jesus "because they saw the signs he had performed by healing the sick". All through his earthly ministry, large crowds followed Jesus. Everywhere he went his teaching, works and lifestyle drew crowds to him. In this passage, the crowd that pressed on him by the Sea of Galilee was at least five thousand strong. Women and children were probably not counted. Jesus soon realized that the crowd was hungry. The people who followed him had done so without bringing along any *mealie meal, matoke, gari* or *kenkey* (meals made from maize or cassava).

Only a young lad had followed Jesus fully prepared for any emergency related to the stomach. His mother or whoever was responsible for him had equipped him with a good lunch box consisting of five small loaves of barley bread and two small fish. By the standards of our modern-day faith generation, this boy would be considered "out of sync" with Jesus. How could he follow Jesus without expecting a miracle? How could he have been more concerned about "daily bread" than the message of the kingdom? He must have been faithless not to expect a miracle from the Master himself.

Well, it turned out that the boy who came prepared was part of the miracle for the day. It was his little lunch that Jesus distributed to feed the whole crowd. They all ate until they were full; the leftovers filled twelve baskets. The people were so impressed with this miraculous sign that they began to say, "Surely this is the Prophet who is come into the world." If they had had their way, they would have forcefully made Jesus their king, but he withdrew to be alone for a while. News of the feeding of the crowd spread across the region, and boatloads of people from Tiberias came looking for Jesus. On arriving at the place where the miracle had happened, they were not a little disappointed by the fact that Jesus had moved on. Back into their boats they went and proceeded to Capernaum, where Jesus had joined his disciples after his withdrawal from the crowd.

When the people eventually caught up with him, Jesus knew exactly why they had come after him. "Very truly I tell you, you are looking for me, not because you saw the signs I performed but because you ate the loaves and had your fill" (John 6:26). He then warned them, "Do not work for the food that spoils, but for food that endures to eternal life, which the Son of Man will give you. On him God the Father has placed his seal of approval."

Taken aback, they asked, "What must we do to do the works God requires?" Jesus responded, "The work of God is this: to believe in the one he has sent." They soon went back to their original motive by reminding Jesus that their ancestors ate manna in the desert and quoted Scripture to enlighten him, "He gave them bread from heaven to eat." Jesus kept urging them to focus on him. He declared that he is the bread of life, and those who believe in him will never be hungry or thirsty again. He pointed to himself as the reality that brings lasting satisfaction. But the crowd would have none of that kind of bread. They wanted more of the physical bread like the manna God gave through

Moses and like the bread that had fed the crowd the previous day. In their commitment to the bread that gives only a temporary benefit, they rejected Jesus' offer to satisfy their spiritual hunger. The crowd was more than disappointed. Why did Jesus have to remind them that their fathers died despite eating manna in the desert? Why should he claim to be the bread that gives eternal life?

They complained, saying, "This is a hard teaching, who can accept it?" (John 6:60) Not long after, most of them drifted back to wherever they had come from. They quit following him. These people completely misunderstood Jesus and his mission. They discovered he was not ready to satisfy their demand for temporary material blessings. Some realised that he emphasised faith in himself, and not just good deeds to get into the kingdom of God. Most of them decided Jesus was not going to be the conquering Messiah-King they expected. So they turned their backs on him.

The "Health and Wealth" Gospel Preachers

In many ways, thousands of those who follow Jesus today are no different from the crowd in John 6. Like that crowd, we want to follow him and possibly proclaim him king. but our motives are also as suspect as those of that crowd. Many people follow Jesus today not because he is the bread of life but because they see him as the means to material prosperity. There are thousands of drifters who move from one church to the next and from a "crusade" to a "revival" meeting in search of material blessings. However, while Jesus pointed those who followed him for bread to eternal life, there are many preachers and teachers today who tell the seekers what they want to hear. These itinerant preachers propagate a "health and wealth" gospel, a gospel of material prosperity without pointing them to the cross of Christ for eternal life. The result is a generation of Christians who cannot see that the "kingdom of God is not eating and drinking, but righteousness and peace and joy in the Holy Spirit!" (Rom 14:17, NKJV) In Nigeria, it is not an overstatement to say that the most popular gospel says, "Seek ye first the things of this world and their fullness, and the kingdom of God shall be added unto you" rather than "Seek ye first the kingdom of God and his righteousness, and all these things shall be added unto you."

What was once covetousness is now "possessing your inheritance by faith". So we have thousands of Christians who want Abraham's blessings but not his trials. The gospel of greed is always okay for those who ignore the real mission of Jesus. For when they stand face to face with the real Jesus and his teaching, they, like the crowd in Capernaum are bound to say, "This is a hard teaching, who can accept it?" While some two thousand years ago, the Lord drove out profit-makers from the temple saying, "My house will be called a house of prayer but you are making it a den of robbers" (Matt 21:13), many of today's houses of prayer have been taken over by "thieves" lurking there to extort money from the faithful who can be deluded into expecting a hundredfold in return. "Give to God and be blessed a hundredfold" they are told! In fear or in expectation of great returns, the people empty their pockets into the collection bags. In the meantime the "pastor", "bishop" or "apostle" gets richer.

How have we slipped from the simplicity of the gospel of Christ – moderation and an emphasis on contentment – to an excessive pursuit of the things of this world?

Tracing the Roots – Made in the United States of America

A substantial part of what constitutes this trend in Nigeria and some other parts of Africa originated from the United States. Notwithstanding the many positive things that have come or have been imported from the United States – gadgets that are products of America's technological advancement; the commitment to democracy and civil rights; a rich Christian heritage dating back to the 18th century revivals and the 20th century evangelical tradition; and more – the health and wealth gospel is doing harm to the church of Christ. It is easy for the average young African to assume that everything American is God sent. After all, we are told America is "God's own country"! The inscription on the dollar "In God we trust" should not make us assume that everything American is ordained of God. The drive that expanded Coca-Cola worldwide is the same that extends Hollywood and its legacy of contagious violence, pornography and other dehumanising attributes to the remotest parts of the world. We seem to drink in the health and wealth gospel with as much enthusiasm as we do Coca-Cola, Campbell's soup and Hollywood.

The problem is not just what America exports. It is the gullibility with which we embrace everything that flows from that land. It is no longer news that the ambition of many young Africans is to migrate to America where the good life is believed to be. Were there to be another slave trade, many would gladly volunteer to be shipped abroad.

Sadly, too many Africans have embraced what discerning Americans have found unacceptable. As a number of American commentators have observed, the health and wealth gospel is nothing but the American dream re-clothed in biblical garments. According to Don McConnell, "The doctrine of prosperity is a gross example of the church's cultural accommodation to the worldly values of American materialism."[1] Warren Wiersbe identifies this "success gospel" as one that is perfectly suited to American society that "worships health, wealth and happiness."[2] According to Gordon Fee:

> American Christianity is rapidly being infected by an insidious disease, the so-called "wealth and health" gospel – although it has a very little of the character of the gospel in it. In its more brazen forms ... it simply says, "Serve God and get rich" ... in its more respectable – but pernicious forms it builds fifteen million-dollar Crystal Cathedrals to the glory of affluent suburban Christianity.[3]

In their pursuit of materialism and upward mobility, the prosperity televangelists who export this gospel have found convenient ways of manipulating Scripture to justify their greed and expensive lifestyles.

In his book, *Defeating the Dragons of the World*, Stephen D. Eyre rightly identifies this cultural trend that has invaded the church as the "Dragon of Materialism":

> The Dragon of Materialism leads us to become pre-occupied with the material side of life. All our time, energy and thoughts are focussed in the physical aspects of life. We became practical materialists. We know that there is more to life, but the way we live shows that we have adopted the creed of the Dragon of Materialism, "Matter is all that matters."[4]

The impact of this dragon is felt from the campus to the larger American society:

> Students no longer have that internal drive for some bigger cause. The issues on campus today revolve around good times, good grades and hopes for finding a good job ... But such an approach to life is not limited to the campus. The campus is just a reflection of our society as a whole. The craving for personal peace and affluence afflicts us all. Even while the starving millions in Africa, the oppression of apartheid and other disasters all tug at our consciences, the message of the media, the pressure of the job and the battle of the budget (personal and national) – in short, the institutions of our world and our own perceived needs sing a siren's song of superficiality. The message of God's offer of life to a fallen world loses its impelling force and the church, like the rest of the culture, is pulled into a treadmill life going nowhere.[5]

The reality is that materialism becomes not only a dragon but also a god that demands our attention and loyalty. In his *Idols of our Time*, Bob Gourdzwaard says of this trend:

> We know from Scripture that both persons and societies can put their faith in things and forces which their own hands have made. In their pursuit of prosperity, salvation, health, protection and so forth, people sooner or later create gods. But gods never leave their makers alone. Because people put themselves in a position of dependence on their gods, invariably, the moments come when those things or forces gain the upper hand.[6]

Thus the prosperity gospel emerging out of the North American social-economic cultural context and empowered by the medium of television should not be seen as anything less than materialism become a dragon and idol that has enslaved its makers. However, in all fairness, the average American earns his prosperity through the sweat of hard work – with the exception of those who hit the lottery jackpot. But the televangelists want instant wealth through the manipulation of other people, under the guise of faith. Jim Bakker, founder of PTL ministry and Heritage

USA, whose empire collapsed in 1987, has since repented. He conceded that PTL had become a 1980s-style tower of Babel to make a name for himself. In his words, "I allowed the PTL ministry to grow in such a way that the buildings at Heritage USA became almost more important than the message of Jesus Christ. My vision was so important that I worked day and night to keep this *monster* alive".[7]

Among the prominent Americans whose prosperity gospel has influenced the church in Africa are Oral Roberts and his son Richard Roberts with their "seed-faith" gospel. Then we have Kenneth and Gloria Copeland with their "hundredfold return" heresy; John Avanzini who markets a super-rich Jesus; and Frederick Price, who claims that the reason he rides in a Rolls Royce is because he is following in Jesus' steps.[8] Then there are Morris Cerullo and Robert Tilton. Other faith teachers closely associated with this tradition are Kenneth Hagin, Fred Price and Paul Couch, the owner of Trinity Broadcasting Network.

The "Seed-faith" Principle

The greatest influence on the emergence of the prosperity gospel in Nigeria is Oral Roberts whose teaching was embraced and taught by Bishop Benson Idahosa – the undisputed father of the prosperity gospel in Nigeria. Oral Robert's seed-faith principle is based on a thought that he says became crystal clear to him one day in the early fifties. The thought was, "Whatever you can conceive, and believe, you can do."[9] According to Roberts:

> I could feel my inner man begin to stir. I could feel myself standing up on the inside. I became excited as I began to see the meaning of the idea that God brought into my mind, *whatever you can conceive, and believe, you can do!* I saw God had first conceived the world and man. I saw He had believed. And what faith it was! God had believed in man enough to create him with the power to choose good and evil, to live positively or negatively, to believe or to doubt, to respond to God or to denounce Him.[10]

With this thought, Oral Roberts was convinced that, "everything God does starts with a seed planted,"[11] that "only what you give can God multiply back. If you give nothing, and even if God were to multiply it, it would still be nothing."[12] Our tithes or offerings to God are therefore *seed faith*. Out of this, Oral Roberts built his doctrine of seed-faith, backing it with Genesis 8:22, which says that:

> As long as the earth endures seedtime and harvest, cold and heat, summer and winter, day and night will never cease.

We receive back from God only as much as we sow as seeds. Therefore seed-faith involves seed-giving. Oral Roberts argues that our seed-giving is multiplied and given back to us so that we have "meat" in our houses – or more than enough for our personal needs. He developed this idea further into his "expect-a-miracle" principle, which stresses that insurmountable problems can all be solved through seed-giving. God essentially becomes an insurance agent in whom one invests with expectation of returns.

Oral Roberts used radio and TV shows to attract people to give to his ministry. Through his "Expect a Miracle" programme and his books, he marketed his seed-faith principle. Eventually, he began issuing special handkerchiefs to be used as "prayer cloths" and a "point of contact" for miracles. Of course, those in need of them have to send a donation. According to Peter Elvy in *Buying Time,* Oral Roberts also published a special edition of the Bible with a 259-page commentary in which the seed-faith principle was the interpretative paradigm. About the commentary, Oral Roberts said:

> It is not for sale. God impressed me to send it as a gift to everyone who makes a seed-faith commitment of $120 for the ongoing work at the city of Faith Medical and Research Center where medicine and prayer are combined for the healing of millions.[13]

Patti Roberts, formerly married to Oral Roberts' son Richard Roberts, is right in likening her former father-in-law's tactics to Johann Tetzel's practice of selling indulgences, in her book, *Ashes to Gold*.[14] The only difference is that whereas Tetzel offered salvation in exchange for money, Oral Roberts appealed to people's needs through his seed-faith principle.

I was in the United States at the peak of the televangelist scandals. In January 1987, Oral Roberts told his followers that if he did not raise eight million dollars by March, God was going to take his life by the first of April. Both Christian and secular media carried this announcement. He was eventually rescued from being taken home by God by a gambler. Oral Roberts was so carried away by this method of fund raising that he at times even resorted to threats. At a conference in 1992, Roberts is said to have uttered these words:

> Someone will be watching this ministry on the air, who promised a large sum [of money] to God. And you act like you have given it, but you did not pay it. You are so close to lying to the Holy Ghost, that within days you will be dead unless you pay the price God said. And somebody here is getting the message. You are on the edge of lying to the Holy Ghost. Don't lie to the Holy Ghost. The prophet has spoken.[15]

The "Seed-faith" Heresy

By asserting that "whatever you can conceive, and believe, you can do", Oral Roberts fails to acknowledge firstly that he is not God who can conceive "whatever", and secondly, that biblical faith is not about "conceiving whatever"; it is about confidence in God to accomplish what he wills. Although Oral Roberts and others who follow his seed-faith doctrine will have us believe that God is obligated to repay a multiplied version of one's "investment", we know of several people in the Bible whom God blessed and provided for even though they had not offered any seed-faith giving to him. Consider Abraham and Solomon. What seed-faith did Abraham offer God? God blessed Abraham and made him prosperous long before God asked him to sacrifice Isaac. As for Solomon, he neither gave nor asked God for material wealth before God gave him riches beyond measure.

Thirdly, the seed-faith doctrine contradicts the truth that our giving to God is first and foremost an act of worship. We worship him by offering our lives and resources to him as gifts with no strings attached. God is not an insurance agent who needs our seed-faith investments.

Fourthly, a closer examination of Oral Roberts' interpretation of Galatians 6:7 which he uses as basis for his seed-faith doctrine, reveals that he interprets the verse out of its context. Oral Roberts argues:

> You are a product of seed so am I. Even Jesus is called the seed of David. Jesus talked about an eternal law. "People reap what they sow" (Galatians 6:7). You sow a seed, you reap a harvest. You give a seed, you receive it back multiplied many times.[16]

But Paul's discussion on sowing and reaping in Galatians is not in the context of giving. In the following verses Paul clarified what his message is about: "Those who sow to please their sinful nature, from that nature will reap destruction; those who sow to please the spirit, from the spirit will reap eternal life" (Gal 6:8). Paul is speaking about the discipline a Christian practices that yields a life of faithfulness to God.

The "Hundredfold Return" Heresy

Outdoing Oral Roberts' seed faith is the hundredfold return teaching expounded by people like Gloria and Kenneth Copeland. In her book, *God's Will is Prosperity*, Gloria Copeland writes:

> You give $1 for the Gospel's sake and $100 belongs to you; give $10 and receive $1,000; give $1,000 and receive $100,000. I know that you can multiply, but I want you to see in black and white how tremendous the hundredfold return is ... Give one house and receive hundred houses or one house worth one hundred times as much. Give one airplane and receive one hundred times the value of the airplanes. Give one car and the return would furnish you with a lifetime of cars. In short, Mark 10:30 is a good deal.[17]

Her husband, Kenneth Copeland believes this is the spiritual law of prosperity. This law, according to him, is universal and works for whoever understands it. Such a person must have faith in it and apply it. It is a law set in motion by a positive mental attitude and positive confession. The law of prosperity is related to Copeland's "force of faith" about which he has also written a book. To him, "it is this force of faith which makes the laws of the spirit world function."[18] It is this force of faith that makes Copeland believe that one can have anything he confesses. According to him:

> *You can have what you say!* In fact, what you are saying is exactly what you are getting now. If you are living in poverty and lack and want, change what you are saying. It will change what you have ... Discipline your vocabulary. Discipline everything you do, everything you say, and everything you think to agree with what God does, what God says, and what God thinks. God will be obligated to meet your needs because of His Word ... If you stand firmly on this, your needs will be met.[19]

The Copeland's one hundredfold teaching is based on their literal interpretation of Mark 10:29–30, and is a distortion of Christ's promise to provide a hundredfold return to those who leave behind everything for the kingdom of God. The passage reads:

> Truly I tell you, Jesus replied, "no one who has left home or brothers or sisters or mother or father or children or fields for me and the gospel will fail to receive a hundred times as much in this present age: homes, brothers, sisters, mothers, children and fields – along with persecutions – and in the age to come, eternal life."

In interpreting this verse, the Copelands ignore the mention of persecutions and the warning in Mark 10:25: "It is easier for a camel to go through the eye of a needle than for the rich to enter the kingdom of God". This verse cannot be interpreted in the same literal way as those that promise prosperity. Gloria Copeland says:

> Prosperity is yours! It is not something you have to strive to work toward. You have a title deed to prosperity. Jesus bought and paid for your prosperity just like He bought and paid for your healing and your salvation.[20]

Unfortunately, like many other prosperity teachers, the Copelands have built a doctrine on the basis of texts taken out of context and manipulated to suit their ends.

Televangelists John Avanzini and Morris Cerullo seem to have built on the Copeland's hundredfold heresy. In his book, *Christianity in Crisis,*

Hank Hanegraff observes how the partnership between Cerullo and Avanzini launched them into the hundredfold heresy. According to him:

> Cerullo summoned Avanzini to Aba, Nigeria. There in a hotel room, God supposedly appeared to Avanzini and said, "I'm gonna have signs and wonders follow your ministry". After giving Avanzini a wordy discourse on fundraising techniques, God instructed him to take an offering for Cerullo. As God allegedly put it, "I want you to lay hands on that offering, and I want you to speak hundred-fold increase over that offering – that it will be multiplied back to the giver hundred fold."[21]

As it has happened so many times, the gullible Nigerian audience gave generously in expectation of hundredfold returns in cash, cars, houses etc. They gave so much that Cerullo himself had to stop people from giving more. Cerullo and Avanzini, went back home much richer than they were before embarking on their trip.

To justify further his hunger for physical and material comfort, Avanzini interprets Jesus' words, "Foxes have holes and birds have nests, but the Son of Man has no place to lay his head" (Luke 9:58) as meaning "Foxes have holes in Samaria, birds of the air have nests in Samaria, but I don't have any place to stay tonight in Samaria." According to Avanzini, "In those days there wasn't a Holiday Inn on every corner. So Jesus was forced to go back home to his nice, big house in Jerusalem."[22]

Although I have not verified with other sources, Don McConnell and Hank Hanegraaff say that they have traced the roots of many of these prosperity and faith teachers to the metaphysical cults. According to McConnell:

> The metaphysical cults, particularly New Thought and the Unity School of Christianity, were the first to propagate the idea that God will make rich all those who know "the laws of prosperity" which govern the universe. Through Kenyon, this cultic belief entered the faith movement and was expanded by Kenneth Hagin and the Faith teachers to a degree which even he himself would never have approved.[23]

Ralph Waldo Trine, who was an associate of E. W. Kenyon, advocated the occult practice of visualisation as a means to prosperity. According to him:

> Suggest prosperity to yourself. See yourself in a prosperous condition. Affirm that you will before long be in prosperous condition. Affirm it calmly and quietly but strongly and confidently. Believe it, believe it absolutely. Expect it – keep it continually watered with expectation. You thus make yourself a magnet to attract the things that you desire.[24]

Hank Hanegraaff also says Kenyon's life and ministry were "enormously influenced by such cults as Science of Mind, the Unity School of Christianity, Christian Science, and New Thought metaphysics".[25]

This then is the background to the health and wealth gospel, otherwise called the prosperity gospel, which has become so popular in many African countries.

The Prosperity Gospel in Africa

It was in the 1980s that the prosperity gospel crept into the charismatic movement in Africa, particularly in Kenya, Nigeria and Ghana. The leading advocates in West Africa were Bishop (later Archbishop) Benson Idahosa of Nigeria and Rev. (Dr.) (now Archbishop) Nicholas Duncan Williams of Ghana, and later Bishop David Oyedepo of Nigeria. Idahosa is believed to have been its first apostle and the one who transported it through his evangelistic crusades across the cities of Africa. I have seen for myself that these men, like their American mentors, live very affluent lives characterised by flamboyant attire, expensive cars and big mansions. They want to live out the American dream in Africa. The philosophy of their gospel seems to be, "Seek ye first the things of this world, and the kingdom of God shall be added unto you."

The Interpretation of the Offering Time in Some Churches

In the past the central part of the worship service was the proclamation of the word. Today in many churches the centrepiece is the "offering time". Not a few churches have specially skilled and designated people to be masters of this significant ceremony. The popular saying is "Offering time is blessing time", not least because for many it is viewed as investment time. It is often regarded as a time to sow, while looking forward to significant returns. The Bible itself is often twisted to back the centrality of offering time and in some churches there is a mini-sermon to urge the congregation to give. Quite often there can be as many as five or six different collections taken in a single service. For example, in September 2008 I was at a church in Lagos where there were six different collections for various purposes, including freedom from fear. One cannot but feel that the flock are being fleeced.

Like their mentors in America, these preachers use Scripture passages to persuade their members to part with their money. The most popular verse is Luke 6:38:

> Give, and it will be given to you. A good measure, pressed down, shaken together, and running over, will be poured into your lap. For with the measure you use, it will be measured to you.

This verse is quoted with relish and is often backed up by a mini-sermon on the benefits of giving. Its use is, however, often not faithful to the text or the context, which is Jesus' teaching on love and mercy and how we relate to and treat others. The paragraph begins:

> Do not judge, and you will not be judged. Do not condemn, and you will not be condemned. Forgive and you will be forgiven.

Following God's example, love and mercy should produce a hesitation in judging others, as believers realise that God will treat them in the way they have treated others. The passage is first and foremost about relationships, and about not treating others or judging them in the way we do not want to be judged, for in this regard "with the measure you use, it will be measured to you" (Mark 4:14).

The passage is therefore not about giving to God financially and expecting returns. It has more to do with loving and forgiving as well as being of service without expecting anything in return. This has, however, been twisted to imply that God will return double or hundredfold whatever one gives in an offering. It is common for several collections to be taken in a single service. Songs like "I Am a Millionaire" and "Let the Poor Say I Am Rich" become popular in anticipation of God's reward with material blessings. Positive confession is encouraged for good health, wealth and other blessings.[26]

Very few people who use this passage as a basis for motivating or mobilising people to give have observed that it is preceded by some very strong words of the Lord Jesus Christ on wealth and resources. For example, in the very same chapter Jesus says:

> But woe to you who are rich, for you have already received your comfort. Woe to you who are well fed now, for you will go hungry. Woe to you who laugh now, for you will mourn and weep. (Luke 6:24–25)

The appeal to give has had a significant impact on average members of various churches, particularly those in struggling situations who go to church "expecting their miracles". People have lost confidence in the countless government promises to eradicate poverty by this or that date, all of which have passed and left them poorer than before the promises were made. Non-governmental organisations seem to spend more money on their fuel-guzzling four-wheel-drive vehicles than on the desperate situations they are expected to relieve. In response, many have turned to the church as the place to find relief from poverty. Perhaps it is the realities of our context that make the desire for financial self-reliance or success so contagious and all-consuming. People are familiar with acute poverty, with low (non-living) wages creating dependency and with high inflation driving up costs.

The situation has definitely contributed to the rapid growth of this "prosperity" or "health and wealth" gospel in the African church as well as in other parts of the world. Although it was initially closely associated with the charismatic renewal and churches or ministries related to it, this "gospel" has since spread significantly beyond these lines.

Benson Idahosa even taught that poverty is a sin! He introduced the concept of God being bigger than small denominations of money. Speaking in terms of Nigerian currency, he would say, "My God is bigger than 10 naira", and so on. He argued that since all the money in the world belongs to God, he was entitled to get it by any means. It doesn't matter what the source of money was, as long as it came in.

This philosophy enabled him to build a multi-million-dollar enterprise called the Idahosa World Outreach, the Church of God Mission, and the Miracle Centre. In Benin City he operated a medical centre and a high school and planned to start a university.

These African teachers, like their mentors, focus on miracles, emphasising healing and deliverance from ill health, poverty and demons as the heart of their gospel. Some have gone even further and forbidden the use of medical drugs, arguing for divine healing only, because they attribute all suffering to the devil. When death strikes, it is believed to be of the devil and some churches are even known to avoid burying the dead. They do not conduct funeral services.

This obsession with materialism has since spread to several other pastors and bishops. Idahosa inspired the two leading prosperity preachers in Lagos who I referred to as having acquired aircraft "for the purpose of evangelism". While there are countless lesser lights, we shall consider only the leading disciple of Oral Roberts, John Avanzini and Benson Idahosa, the man who is rapidly spreading the gospel of wealth and health from one African country to the other. He is David Oyedepo.

David Oyedepo

Combining all he has learnt from his mentors with his own creativity, David Oyedepo has expanded the Winners Chapel and the Word of Faith Bible Institute beyond Nigeria to other parts of Africa. By his own admission he believes in sweat-less success and teaches his followers that "the knowledge and the practice of the truth make you a sweat-less winner."[27] His essential philosophy is that life is meant to be a smooth cruise, free of all struggles and full of material wealth. "Not all winners sweat to win. Sweating is a curse. It symbolises struggles."

Oyedepo believes poverty is a curse and is self-made. He uses Malachi 3:6–9 to establish this. According to him, poverty "comes largely as a result of a wilful act of disobedience to the law of abundance by the believers."[28] Are we therefore to assume that all those who live in abject poverty in various parts of Africa are reaping the rewards of wilful disobedience?

Oyedepo says God has given him a mission to eradicate poverty. He believes that his primary call and mission is to make people rich.

According to him, God gave him the covenant hammer to break all chains of poverty. "I took hold of it and declared, 'I can never be poor!' That was not an empty confession; I knew what I was saying, and what had been delivered to me. It has never disappointed me once! Friend, it is time to begin to hunger and thirst for this same hammer to be delivered to you."[29] He writes about how he received this call:

> I remember very clearly, in 1987, I was in the United States of America, attending a meeting when the Lord said to me, "Get down home quick and make my people rich." They were very strong, compelling and powerful words. So I abandoned everything I was doing, I cancelled all engagements, and rushed down home immediately.[30]

Members of the Living Faith or Winners Chapel deal with poverty and other inconveniences in many ways. Miracles are, however, the key, and these are stimulated by the use of consecrated objects. Across West Africa, from Lagos to Freetown, people have been taught that such objects possess supernatural powers in themselves. David Oyedepo even alleges that

> the anointing oil is not a chemical product. It is the Spirit of God mysteriously put in a bottle, mysteriously designed to communicate the power of God bodily. It is the power of God in your hand, in the person of the Holy Spirit, to humiliate Satan. It is the power of God placed in a tangible form in the hand of man, to make an open show of the devil.[31]

Many followers of Oyedepo believe this and see the oil (usually olive oil) as the solution to their problems. Believing that it is powerful in itself, they use it as a protective device, anointing their television sets, cars and the four corners of their homes for protection against thieves.

Related to this is the belief that when blackcurrant juice is added to water and prayed over by the bishop, it becomes the blood of Jesus. It is then placed at strategic points in a house, particularly on doorposts and windows, to provide protection from demonic attacks. It is also used to deliver people from oppression, poverty, sickness and so on.

White handkerchiefs that have been prayed over by the bishop are sometimes referred to as "bishop's mantles" and are believed to be so powerful that some members hang them at the entrance to their offices or shops to attract customers. Others hang them on their door post to drive away demons.

There are also other ways to deal with poverty and nagging problems. The Living Faith or Winners Chapel has a monthly foot-washing service in which the bishop washes the members' feet in order to wash away poverty and problems and to deliver them from oppression. It is believed that members who dip their feet into the water put on iron feet that will enable them walk on their mountains and high places. They will also walk into prosperity and find favour.

The idea of supernatural powers residing in objects and of shortcuts to the good things of life is not original to Oyedepo. Oral Roberts also marketed special Bibles and handkerchiefs. Marilyn Hickey specialised in offering prayer cloths, ceremonial breastplates and ropes as points of contact for miracles.[32]

It may not be too clear how many people Oyedepo has made rich, but there is no doubt he himself has become extremely rich. He started his Winners Chapel with Living Faith Ministries in Kaduna and then moved to Lagos where his World Mission Centre was built for at least 400 million naira (then about $5 million US). His church building seats at least 8,000 per session. He runs three major services on Sundays, which attract at least 30,000 people. He has a multimillion naira press called Dominion Publishing House. In addition to his fleet of expensive cars, he also has a small jet, which he said he bought for the purpose of evangelism. Most of these were bought with the regular tithes and offerings, that are strictly collected from his followers. They are made to believe that the more you give, the more God offers you in return.

Oyedepo believes in talking big about money and wealth. Most of the more than forty books that he has written deal with material prosperity and good health. They include *Covenant Wealth, Breaking Financial Hardship, Success Buttons, Born to Win, The Miracle Seed, Keys to Divine Health, Anointing for Breakthrough* and *The Mystery of the Anointing Oil*. In *Breaking Financial Hardship* he writes:

> Friend there is no place your mouth cannot take you to. When you talk mediocrity it will become your garment and when you talk lack you will have it until you become lack yourself ...

> If you want to have a living financial experience, speak life to your finances.[33]

Oyedepo has fully embraced Oral Roberts' seed-faith concept. Giving is an investment in one's own future.[34] Tithing is divine insurance "against destruction in whatever form". He assures his followers that if they do not pay their tithes, they will be harassed by devouring rats: "Frequent car breakdowns, losses, sickness and so on are all manifestations of the devourer."[35]

For Oyedepo, money is the answer to all things. It is even a defence against being arrested for preaching the gospel. He says:

> Some preachers in Nigeria have been arrested over and over again for preaching in some places. But, some others have gone to preach in the same place and they gave them police security. Why? One has defence, while the other hasn't. Money answers all things. That is why God has designed wealth for his people so He can establish them in dominion.[36]

Oyedepo does not hide the sources of his convictions. In his books he frequently refers to the "successes" and teachings of his heroes. Apart from Oral Roberts, he mentions Kenneth Copeland who has an airstrip where his jet lands every morning and who has given away three jets. John Avanzini is also his hero. There is no doubt that with his combination of positive thinking and confession, he aspires to be as wealthy as his American heroes!

Like Avanzini, Oyedepo markets a rich Jesus. His Jesus:

> has so much that He needed a treasure to keep His money. He ate whatever He wanted and whenever He desired it. He has a place that commanded envy because John's disciples, who went to see where he lived, never returned to their Master.[37]

The sale of olive oil, which he believes is an anointed key to wealth and health, as well as "holy mantels" and the like are part of the ministry of the Winners Chapel. He has also started a chain of Bible schools, the Word of Faith Bible Institute (WOFBI), to popularise his teaching. To date there are Winners Chapels in Nigeria, Kenya, Tanzania, Ethiopia, Uganda and Ghana.

In May 1996 I was in Dar es Salaam, Tanzania. Some friends invited me to come and listen to some new teaching in town. They said, "Come and hear what some strange Nigerians are teaching, then tell us what you make of it." So I went with them to a theatre where a lunch-hour meeting was taking place. On the platform was "the man of God" who declared,

> I can't see anything your mouth declares that will not happen ... If you have HIV/AIDS, declare to cancel the diagnosis. Open your mouth and declare a change. God will confirm it. ... If you need promotion and they don't promote you, declare with your mouth, 'If they don't promote me, no one else will be promoted'. Everything is by declaration! ... Release the word to anything that stands in your way! There is power in the spoken word."

His teaching was punctuated by shouts of "Amen!" We could see that his audience was being carried along, except for a few whose expressions clearly indicated that this was a new teaching. The teacher or preacher then suggested how anyone who needed promotion could act in faith to get it. He suggested that they draft a letter of appointment, anoint it with oil, sneak into the boss's office, lay it on his desk and declare by faith, "I receive my promotion in Jesus name". He assured the audience that the promotion would come.

It did not take me long to know that this preacher came from the Winners Chapel and believed in sweat-less victory and a storm-free life. He made references to his bishop and prayed in the name of the God of his bishop. He offered handkerchiefs and "anointing oil" for sale. These were to be taken to those who were sick at home and in the villages for their healing.

Another Gospel

The health and wealth gospel is not biblical and must be shunned as "another gospel" on many grounds. Firstly, as we have discussed, the seed-faith principle on which it is based in unbiblical. It espouses a view about giving, whether of tithes or offerings, as primarily an investment rather than an act of worship. Thus it leads people to give with wrong motives, expecting special returns from God. The person who gives to God appears to be the one in charge, because it is his or her measure of investment that dictates God's response. It seems that human beings take the initiative and God responds. This contradicts all that the Bible teaches about God taking the initiative to save us and worship being our response to him.

Secondly, this "gospel" gives undue emphasis to our earthly inheritance, here and now in material form. Pursuit of this is contrary to biblical faith and blurs our vision and understanding of God. Stephen Eyre has put it well:

> Materialism blunts a living faith. A vibrant sense of the presence of God becomes dead orthodoxy. The reality of the Christian life becomes a shadow. Our experience of life in Christ becomes hollow. Our knowledge of God becomes empty. If we can't see it, taste it, smell it or measure it, then we doubt that it's real, therefore, we come to doubt that God is real.[38]

Thirdly, those who teach this gospel have misunderstood Jesus and his mission. While Jesus was not destitute, we know from Scripture that he was not as prosperous as the health and wealth teachers make him out to be. His home situation was modest. We know his parents did not have the means to avoid his being born in a stable, and had to lay him in a manger. We know that when his parents went to the temple to dedicate him, all they could give as offering was a pair of doves instead of a lamb and dove as required by the law (Luke 2:21; Lev 12:6). We also know that in his ministry Jesus often depended on the resources of other people because he did not have any of his own. He taught from a borrowed boat, rode into Jerusalem on a borrowed donkey, ate the Passover meal with his disciples in a borrowed room and was buried in a borrowed tomb.

Jesus did not preach or teach a prosperity gospel. In fact, when Jesus did talk about material possessions, he warned his disciples to "Watch out! Be on your guard against all kinds of greed; life does not consist in an abundance of possessions" (Luke 12:15). He also warned against the deceitfulness of wealth (Matt 13:22), referred to it as "unrighteous mammon" (Luke 16:9, NKJV), and warned the Pharisees who loved money that "what people value highly is detestable in God's sight" (Luke 16:15).

When money becomes an end in itself, it has a tendency to compete for our loyalty that belongs to God. It can easily become an idol that rules our lives. This is why Jesus warns against relating to money as we relate to God.

> No one can serve two masters. Either you will hate the one and love the other or you will be devoted to the one and despise the other. You cannot serve both God and money." (Luke 16:13)

The health and wealth gospel contradicts all these warnings of Jesus.

There are few people today who can speak as authoritatively as Bakker on the prosperity gospel. Prior to the PTL scandal, his ministry had a $30-million payroll and more than 2,200 employees. In his 647-page book entitled *I Was Wrong* Bakker confesses his sins.[39] Far from what he used to be, Bakker now teaches about sacrifice and the cost of discipleship. In an interview Bakker says:

> While I was in prison, the Lord showed me He wanted me to study the words of Christ in the Bible. So I began to write out in longhand every word that Christ spoke. I spent two years doing this. I wanted to know Christ and everything He said. And as I began to absorb the teachings of Christ, it changed my life. Sometimes I would be moved to study 16 hours a day.[40]

After his years of study what did Baker discover about Jesus concerning wealth?

> While I studied Jesus' words, I couldn't find anywhere in the Bible where He said anything good about money. And this started to prick my heart. Luke 6:24 says, "Woe to you who are rich." Jesus talked about the "deceitfulness of riches" in Mark 4:19. Jesus told us not to lay up treasures on earth in Matthew 6:24. In Luke 12:15, He said: "Watch out, be on your guard against all kinds of greed. A man's life does not consist in the abundance of his possessions."[41]

Fourthly, the lifestyle of those who teach this gospel does not reflect biblical standards. One of the requirements for leaders and ministers is that they should not be "greedy for money" (Titus 1:7, NKJV; 1 Pet 5:2). Jesus told his disciples that "workers deserve their wages" (Luke 10:7), but he did not encourage covetousness or exploitation of people. The lifestyle of prosperity teachers is in sharp contrast with the life of early disciples like the Apostle Paul who could say:

> I have not coveted anyone's silver or gold or clothing. You yourselves know that these hands of mine have supplied my own needs and the needs of my companions. In everything I did, I showed you that by this kind of hard work we must help the weak, remembering the words the Lord Jesus himself said: "It is more blessed to give than to receive." (Acts 20:33–35)

Even from the Old Testament, which is often used by prosperity teachers, we have much to learn from the testimonies of godly leaders as regards material possessions and integrity. Abraham was careful not to covet other people's riches to enhance his own prosperity (Gen 14:22–23). At the end of his service, Samuel gave an account of his stewardship by declaring before all Israel:

> Here I stand. Testify against me in the presence of the Lord and his anointed. Whose ox have I taken? Whose donkey have I taken? Whom have I cheated? Whom have I oppressed? From whose hand have I accepted a bribe to make me shut my eyes? If I have done any of these things, I will make it right." (1 Sam 12:3)

The people's response was "You have not cheated or oppressed us … You have not taken anything from anyone's hand" (1 Sam 12:4).

Fifthly, the core of the health and wealth gospel departs from the core of the gospel of Christ, whose centre is the cross. It is a "gospel" without the cross, and therefore no gospel at all. It never says, "Whoever wants to be my disciple must deny themselves and take up their cross daily and follow me" (Luke 9:23). Nor does it ever say, "Unless your righteousness surpasses that of the Pharisees and teachers of the law, you will certainly not enter the kingdom of heaven" (Matt 5:20).

This gospel never says: "Anyone who looks at a woman lustfully has already committed adultery with her in his heart" (Matt 5:28), or "in this world you will have trouble. But take heart! I have overcome the world" (John 16:33).

Here on earth there will always be "a time to mourn" as there are also times to dance. There will be times to weep as there will be times to laugh. Christ did not pray for God to take us out of this world but prayed that he should protect us from the evil one (John 17:15).

Those who embrace the prosperity gospel have learnt to read the Bible selectively. They embrace, "a time to be born" but reject any reference to "a time to die". They confess that there is "a time to laugh" but deliberately avoid mentioning "a time to mourn" (Eccl 3:2–4). Even though these are realities of our earthly pilgrimage, in the name of being "overcomers", those who embrace this gospel think of those who suffer or weep as being either sinful or lacking in faith. While we must not go out of our way to seek pain or disease, pretending that they are unreal is nothing but escapism.

It is self-delusion to think one can live in Africa and cruise through life without storms. From the days of our forefathers to contemporary times, we have survived by hard work and sweat. We have been and are still surrounded by pain and disease and, in many countries, hunger. Our forefathers experienced all of these, yet many lived to a ripe old age. Many do the same today, including my grandmother who lived to be over 100 years old. How can we think that we will be delivered from these realities simply because we follow Jesus? In most parts of Africa, those who are completely free from the travails of pain, hunger and poverty are those who have become permanent residents in cemeteries.

In our context, being wealthy also does not necessarily mean a painless passage through life. If you are wealthy and neatly suited but stuck in rush hour traffic around the Tetteh Quarshie Roundabout in Accra, or on the Ibadan Expressway in Nigeria or on the Ngong Road in Nairobi, no matter how wealthy or neatly suited you are, there's not much you can do but sweat it out even if you are in an air-conditioned car.

How does the prosperity gospel deal with a widow who has lost an only child? How does it deal with the countless Christian women who have died in childbirth? What has it to say to the wife of an ECOMOG soldier who waits at the airport all night for returning troops to bring a letter from her husband, only to receive news of his death? What has it to say to the wife who waits and waits, receiving nothing while others are eagerly tearing open envelopes, and goes home not knowing whether her husband is alive or not? What has this gospel got to say to a ten-year-old whose parents are killed in a conflict he or she doesn't understand? And what has it to say to the refugees and destitute of Southern Sudan,

Sierra Leone, Liberia, Rwanda, Burundi or the Congo? Are all those who have suffered this way faithless or sinful? Did they all lose out because they failed to use the prescribed formula? If this gospel has nothing to say to them, its silence speaks very loudly.

The stress on miraculous deliverance from the ailments that beset our daily lives has led some to adopt a lifestyle of lying. It is considered unspiritual to admit, "I have a headache." It is more spiritual to confess, "I am healed" and deny the reality rather than dealing with it. Rather than admit that one has a neck or back pain, it is better to "confess" that "I am strong". To admit that the opposite is true is considered unspiritual.

This gospel of ease is silent on pain and suffering because it has no theology for it. All things related to discomfort, pain, suffering, poverty and death are considered to be of the devil and are therefore to be rejected. The underlying assumption is a misreading of Romans 8:28 to mean "only good things happen to those that are in Christ Jesus" or that "Christians are not to suffer". A very popular song among groups and churches that have embraced this theology goes like this:

> Me I no go suffer, I no go beg for bread.
> Me I no go suffer, I no go beg for bread.
> God (of miracles), na my papa o, na my mama o;
> Me I no go suffer, I no go beg for bread.

It is sung in services and meetings to reinforce the belief that since God is my father and mother, I will never suffer or beg for bread. This conviction is reinforced by a distorted assumption about suffering. Is it really true that only good things happen to those who are in Christ Jesus?

Now, Romans 8:28 is a very beautiful verse, it says, "And we know that in all things God works for the good of those who love him, who have been called according to his purpose." These words are so clear; yet many of us think they means that *only* good things will happen to those who love God. We need to ask what the "all things" are within the context of the verse. Some of those things are listed in verses 35 to 39, and they include trouble, hardship, persecution, famine, nakedness, danger and the sword. Paul is not saying we shall escape these things but that even if we go through them, God can use them for good in his overall plan for those who love him. He goes on to say that none of these things can separate us from the love of God.

Another related assumption is that anyone living right with God will never suffer. It is easy to assume that everything should work positively or conveniently for those living right and that only the wicked suffer. Psalm 1 gives a picture of the righteous prospering in whatever they do and the wicked perishing. So even by picking some verses in the Bible, we may easily come to believe that only the wicked suffer. This is a very strong theme in the Old Testament beginning with Exodus. While the Egyptians suffered from the various plagues, God shielded his people. As long as his people were obedient, God promised to bless and prosper them. Obedience leads to prosperity and disobedience leads to catastrophe. This theme is also strong in Deuteronomy.

> Do what is right and good in the Lord's sight, so that it may go well with you and you may go in and take over the good land that the Lord promised on oath to your ancestors. (Deut 6.18)

But then,

> If you ever forget the Lord your God and follow other gods and worship and bow down to them, I testify against you today that you will surely be destroyed." (Deut 8:19)

This pattern is confirmed by many events. Yet by the time one gets to Psalm 73, David is struggling with the very opposite of this philosophy. He describes the righteous suffering while the wicked prosper. Hear David:

> For I envied the arrogant when I saw the prosperity of the wicked. They have no struggles; their bodies are healthy and strong. They are free from common human burdens; they are not plagued by human ills. (Ps 73:3–5)

David said that he was almost destabilised by this until he entered the house of the Lord. He was not alone in discovering that the wicked do not always suffer or perish in this life. Jeremiah, too, asked, "Why does the way of the wicked prosper? Why do all the faithless live at ease?" (Jer 12:1)

A close study of Scripture will reveal that suffering and even death are not solely the preserve of the wicked. Concerning suffering it states, "the righteous may have many troubles" (Ps 34:19). We discover that even the godly suffer and at times die in their suffering. Joseph lived right but was still sold as a slave and imprisoned for some years, though he was guiltless. Hananiah, Mishael and Azariah (better known as Shadrach, Meshach and Abednego) were thrown into a burning furnace because they would not compromise. And although Paul was a faithful witness and apostle, his record of suffering and hardship surpasses that of many wicked men (2 Cor 11:22–33). Thus we cannot categorically say that those living right will not suffer or die like others. We know from Scripture and contemporary history that many saints have suffered greatly. Physical death is a common experience that does not distinguish between the righteous and the wicked. God in his wisdom has appointed it so.

Some people who are disappointed with God feel he is unfair. Job's wife must have drawn that conclusion when she asked Job to curse God and die. She held God directly responsible for Job's pain. Yet Job did not curse God. His response to her was: "You are talking like a foolish woman. Shall we accept good from God, and not trouble?' (Job 2:10)

This stance taken by Job is not very popular in a day when people believe that once you are a Christian, everything will go right for you. We often think of the book of Job as a treatise on suffering, yet Philip Yancey is correct to say:

> The point of the book is not suffering: "Where is God when it hurts?" The point is faith: "Where is Job when it hurts? How is he responding?"[42]

The health and wealth gospel is therefore nothing less than seduction into a delusion. Warren Wiersbe has summed it up well:

> The success preachers give us a distorted view of God, of the Saviour, of the Christian life and also of the church. According to them, the church of Jesus Christ is a gathering of happy people who are enjoying life. According to my Bible, the church is a gathering of hurting people who are seeking to be holy before God and helpful to a needy world. Yes, there ought to be celebration and joy when the church meets to worship; but there must also be the sharing of burdens, the washing of wounds, and the healing of broken hearts. But according to the success gospel, Christians shouldn't be hurting at all.[43]

To embrace the prosperity gospel is to fall into the peril of the love of money that Paul warned Timothy about (2 Tim 3:1–5). It is to become more earthly-minded than heavenly-minded, forgetting that the kingdom of God is "not of this world" and assuming that it is primarily "a matter of eating and drinking" (Rom 4:17).

Yet this gospel has spread. Through the health and wealth gospel, the church in many parts of the world – Africa, Europe, and even the Middle East as well as nations within Eastern Europe and Asia that were once under the yoke of communism – has been invaded by a celebrity culture that has little space or room for the cross of Jesus Christ. Hence Scripture is twisted and manipulated to accommodate or justify lifestyles that are radically opposed to taking up the cross to follow Jesus. Many people in the church want to live for Jesus without renouncing material greed. The pressure from the red carpet world of celebrities and popular culture seems too hard to resist. For many the quest for a painless life has almost become an obsession that makes the pursuit of happiness an end in itself. People, especially young people, flee from any appearance of discomfort or stress. And to satisfy them, churches have compromised the integrity of Scripture, thus swelling the size of their congregations with drifters in search of the latest shortcuts to the good things in life. Be it in Africa, America, Europe, Asia, Latin America or any other part of the world, the trend is the same – churches have learnt from the consumer culture to be user-friendly.

The Prosperity Gospel and the Challenge of Poverty

Africa has the resources to be the richest continent in the whole world in spite of droughts and other natural disasters that limit production or productivity. Yet significant numbers of our people still live in abject poverty. As the former UN Secretary-General Kofi Annan said:

> For all too many ... life is a continuous struggle against hunger, malnutrition, polluted drinking water, infectious disease, ignorance, oppression and violent conflict.[44]

In much of Africa, the rich are very rich while the poor are very, very poor. This reality fuels an unlimited ascent of greed. Very often those most affected are the younger generation (most of Africa's population is young). When national resources are plundered, it is the future of young people that is compromised. When Nigerian or Angolan oil resources, Cameroonian mahogany or Zambian copper are traded at give-away prices to the highest bidder, it is the future of the younger generation that is being sold.

The inequitable distribution of resources and the resultant gap between the rich and poor in Africa has always been a concern for government and churches. In the past most people looked up to governments for remedy. However that is fast changing as government leadership can hardly meet the needs of the poor. There is growing loss of confidence in political leaders, particularly among young people.

In response, some young people give up and commit suicide, as happened recently with a 21-year-old in South Africa. Insulted by officials and denied a much needed permit to secure work in his own country, this young man committed suicide. Even though the Home Affairs minister wept when she heard of it, her tears were too late to remedy the situation.[45]

Others try to take flight to greener pastures. Thousands of young Africans migrate to Europe or North America because home is no longer safe or offers no hope for a promising future. In 2006 alone, 31,000 illegal immigrants from West Africa are reported to have crossed to Spain's Canary Islands.[46] Issues like these are critical enough to be among the concerns of African churches, but rather than addressing them, the health and wealth gospel fuels them.

Finally, many young people, as well as older people, turn to churches that are, or should be, the custodians of good news to the poor. While some churches are, others are not. This is primarily because, as Schuller suggested many years ago,

> Christianity has impressed many as being largely a social organisation capable of worshipping God and mammon simultaneously, and demanding payments for the symbols of membership, the administration of the sacraments.[47]

There are issues especially with the affluence and lifestyle of some prosperity church leaders. Some are known to be afflicted with greed and shamelessly fleece their flock. Others are known to use the promise of miracles to gain more affluence.

It appears that while many churches claim to be concerned about alleviating the needs of victims of poverty, they have raised another category of victims, whom we could call victims of prosperity. These are people (including some in our African churches) who are so materially prosperous that they have become blind to the needs of others in our society.

While it is important to focus on the victims of poverty, we also need to pay attention to the victims of prosperity, who need to be called to renounce their affluent lifestyle for the sake and benefit of the poor. If the needs of those who are materially poor are to be met, those who are materially affluent need to be better stewards of their resources for the benefit of those less privileged. This, of course, also implies that pastors and bishops need to set an example by living more simply.

All of us, when prosperous and comfortable, tend to be less aware of the plight of others around us. And this is where greed steps in. Lamin Sanneh quotes the Chevalier de Jaucourt, a leading voice of the French Enlightenment, who wrote in 1765 about how "avarice and greed, which ruled the earth, never allowed the cry of humanity on behalf of slaves to be heard."[48] It is easy to say that because we are a people of God or "men of God" we are above such blindness, but as Lamin Sanneh warns, religion itself "could easily be enticed by profits and worldly gain to bend conscience into compliance."[49] There is much work to be done in the area of exhorting the rich to take greater responsibility for the plight of the poor.

Even when disaster strikes, it is easier for the rich to make pledges than fulfil them. The earthquake that hit Haiti at the beginning of 2010 killed between 230,000 and 300,000 persons and left millions of others homeless. The world promised to give $5.3 billion worth of support to Haiti. But six months after the disaster, only 10% of what was pledged had been given, and even that had mainly been in the form of debt cancellation rather than actual cash. At least 1.6 million people were still homeless.[50]

The same magazine that reported on the situation in Haiti carried an unrelated article claiming that "1.3 million unopened yogurt pots are dumped every day in the UK, along with 440,000 ready meals, 5,500 whole chickens, 4.4 million apples, 5.1 million potatoes and 1.6 million bananas.[51] Contrast this waste with the acute need in Haiti. The same paradox is reflected in other parts of the world.

The rich often live and feed on their excesses at the expense of the poor. In a report, Deborah Doane, director of the anti-poverty group known as the World Development Movement, said "Investment banks are making huge profits by gambling on the price of everyday food. This is leaving people in the UK out of pocket and the poorest people in the world are starving."[52] If people in the UK are "out of pocket", you can imagine how price increases affect poor people in the back streets of Timbuktu, Mali, or Zinder, Niger, when it comes to food, homes, medical care and basic education.

The windfall from corporate gambling feeds the indulgence of senior officials of the banks. For example, in the middle of the 2010 recession, Goldman Sachs was planning to pay out almost £6 billion in salaries and bonuses pool, giving staff a 15 per cent pay rise. The percentage may appear small, but it means that the average salary of Goldman bankers would be £356,000 in 2010.[53] Like others of the rich and famous, they would spend much of this on trivial things like entertainment and cosmetics, while the poorest of the poor continue to starve.

Is the Prosperity Gospel Good News for the Poor?

The message of God's kingdom has been called the "Good News". The kingdom is about good news (Luke 4:18). John the Baptist called people to repentance and restoration (Luke 3:10–14). But the prosperity gospel no longer brings good news to the poor. Some women skip going to church because they do not feel they have the right clothes or have nothing to put into any of the multiple collections. Many who do go to church expecting their personal miracle feel a sense of abandonment. As they see others dancing to the front, they feel a sense of diminished self-worth, even though they know that some of those who dance to the front only go through the motions without putting anything into the offering basket. Outside church the pains of poverty give them a diminished sense of dignity as they struggle to make ends meet.

One cannot therefore say the prosperity gospel constitutes "good news" for the poor.

Remembering the Poor

How do we help the church to remember the poor in a context where many do not see the promises made to them by "men of God" fulfilled? We need to take seriously the teaching of the early church:

> James, Cephas and John, those esteemed as pillars, gave me and Barnabas the right hand of fellowship when they recognized the grace given to me. They agreed that we should go to the Gentiles, and they to the Jews. All they asked was that we should continue to remember the poor, the very thing I had been eager to do all along. (Gal 2:9–10)

In his letter to the church at Colossae, Paul writes:

> So put to death the sinful, earthly things lurking within you. Have nothing to do with sexual sin, impurity, lust, and shameful desires. Don't be greedy for the good things of this life, for that is idolatry. (Col 3:5 NLT)

Greed is as much an affliction of the rich as it is of the poor. It takes people who have renounced greed to really remember the needs of the poor.

What more can the church do to focus on the need of the poor? How many churches are really creating opportunities for vocational training or other means of helping the poor? There are issues that require serious thought.

We need to learn to live by the truth that, "Life, in fact, is a pilgrimage from one moment of nakedness to another; so we should travel light and live simply."[54]

9

THE GOD MAN USES

Though the Westminster Catechism asserted that man's chief end was "to glorify God and enjoy Him forever," the modern creed insists that we use God to glorify ourselves and enjoy ourselves forever.

— Michael Horton

How do you view God?

It is very easy for our perception of God to be as sentimental as our individual emotional or circumstantial orientation prescribes. This perception can be shaped quite early. I grew up believing in a God of instant judgement. My image of him was of a supreme, white-haired and transcendent deity sitting on a majestic throne. I never imagined that anyone could see his face since neither human beings nor anything else in creation could see beyond his feet, given how physically exalted he was. I was made to believe he was a stern-faced, long-bearded no-nonsense judge. Who else could send exterminating plagues on the whole nation of Egypt or cause the Israelites to be consumed by fire or serpents in the desert? I grew up listening to thundering Baptist preachers tell of the way that he destroyed 23,000 in a single day for their acts of immorality. And of how he turned a 40-day trek into a 40-year nightmare for the Israelites because of their unbelief. I heard of how he smote Uzzah dead for daring to touch the Ark of the Covenant.

I was scared stiff of this God who speaks in lightning and thunder. It was all too literal for me. I thought I feared my mother's discipline more than anything else in the world – until this image of God grasped me. Once I did something wrong and could not admit it to my mother. For several days, which seemed like years, I felt the eyes of God trailing me everywhere I went and silently thundering in my heart and fragile frame, "You did it." Once, while idling time away on a football field, I lay on my back and stared up at the sky. Playfully, I focused on the sun. It suddenly seemed to me that it took the shape of the biggest eye I had ever seen. It was God hounding me again, ready to shout "Got you!" Therefore, as a kid, I repented many times of sins I had never committed. Being in a Baptist church, that seemed to major in altar calls, I went forward more times than I can remember, "accepting" Jesus as my Saviour over and over again. With this one-sided knowledge of the God of the Old Testament, I knew very little of the love of God that made him send Jesus to die in my place.

Of course many things have since changed. Or have they? After several years of knowing the God of love and his saving grace through Jesus Christ, I was confronted with a different perception of God. This perception is that of the God humans use. When I saw how widespread this understanding of God was, I had to write about him.

The "God" Man Uses[1]

> My soul thirsts for God, for the living God:
> When can I go and meet with God? (Ps 42:2)

Oswald J. Smith wrote a book entitled *The Man God Uses*. The church knows about God using individuals for his divine purposes and glory. But in the days we live in and within the church, the "modern" Christian has invented a "God" he can use. This "God" is supposedly the God and Father of our Lord Jesus Christ, but he is also a being whom people, and particularly some preachers, can use and manipulate for their own ends. This "God" has mass appeal and followership – and for good reasons.

First, he can be ordered, instructed or "commanded" to do whatever we want.[2] When we demand a miracle, he must perform one, for this "God" is expected to give us whatever is demanded of him, regardless of his own desires or will. He is the "prosperity God" who must bless and deliver gifts regardless of our relationship with him. He is not sought for who he is, but for what he has to offer.

Secondly, this "God" has no glory left, for when all is said and done, the focus of attention and "awe" is not "God" but the "man of God" who has "made" God do what the audience wanted. Not only has his glory been stolen, but his other attributes have also been lost. In the pursuit of what he has to offer, there is no room for such "trivial" matters as his holiness or sovereignty.

Thirdly, this "God" hardly cares how his followers live. He is proclaimed as one who winks at ungodliness or double standards in the lives of his promoters and followers. He is content as long as he gets 10% of the commitment, time and resources of his followers, and he does not interfere with other aspects of their lives. Were his standards to be measured by the lifestyles of his followers, he would be found wanting.

For all these reasons, this "God" is not the God and Father of our Lord Jesus Christ. He is a "God" created in the image of sinful human beings. The tragedy is that those who are supposed to know and serve the true living God are proclaiming such a "God". The truth is that many of us really do not know God as he is. If we knew the sovereign God, who does whatever he wills according to the counsel of his will, we would know that he cannot be manipulated. If we knew the high and lofty God who reigns in majesty above the heavens and the earth, as well as in the midst of his people, we would know what reverence and humility are. If we knew that God is holy, our lives would reflect more of his holy nature. What we are and how we live is very much dependent on our knowledge and understanding of God. A sub-Scriptural understanding of God breeds a sub-Scriptural lifestyle among Christians. A. W. Tozer's words still rings true today: "The Christian is strong or weak depending upon how closely he has cultivated the knowledge of God."[3]

J. I. Parker, author of *Knowing God,* is convinced that ignorance of God lies at the root of much of the church's weakness today. In the foreword to his book, he identified two primary trends. One is that "Christian minds have been conformed to the modern spirit: the spirit, that is, that spawns great thoughts of man and leaves room for only small thoughts of God." The second trend is that, "Christian minds have been confused by modern scepticism."[4] These trends continue even after years of quests to understand God and his ways. It appears that many Christian minds are focused on ways of being conformed to and confused by so-called modernism. Hence Packer's observations that, "One can know a great deal about God without much knowledge of him" and that, "One can know a great deal about godliness without much knowledge of God" is as true today as when he first wrote those words more than two and half decades ago.[5]

The contemporary swing from a transcendent God who dwells in the high and lofty place to one who has become our buddy is one of the tragedies of the new churches in Africa. It is strange that in Africa, where we bow prostrate before earthly rulers, kings, and in some cases our parents, we have increasingly lost our sense of awe and reverence before God. Nothing illustrates this better than the way some of us pray. Even though we read in Scripture how the twenty-four elders bow and cast down their golden crowns before God, we dare to lift our heads and hands to give God instructions on how to meet our needs.

What truly converted Christian in any part of Africa did not learn to pray on his or her knees? Who has truly encountered Christ and does not know that he is Lord and his words, not ours, are "yes and amen"? Who has truly learnt to wait upon God, who did not begin with lying prostrate before God in prayer, often in tears, and who has not spent long periods of stillness in his presence?

Today, we have graduated from all that. It is common to see young men with their hands in their pockets, bouncing around a hall claiming to be praying and "commanding" God to do their bidding. We stand before God in postures that would be considered totally disrespectful were we to do the same before our earthly parents. We have lost the art of reverence before God! But this loss of reverence is hardly strange since the understanding some have of God is that he is an errand boy:

> The pop gospel of success tries to make us believe that God's greatest concern is to make us happy, not to make us holy, and that He is more concerned about the physical and the material than he is about the moral and spiritual. The "success god" is a celestial errand boy whose only responsibility is to respond to our every call and make sure that we are enjoying life.[6]

Anyone who wants to grow in knowledge of the true transcendent God must go beyond the "god of my bishop", the "god of my success" and the "god of my prosperity" to encounter him!

In pursuing a God who will serve our interests, we have become ignorant of the qualities that set God apart from us. We have been helped to degenerate in this way by those who have come to teach us that we ourselves are "little gods". We shall deal more with this later, but suffice it to say that this errand boy idea of God is nothing but blasphemy. How can human beings be God or little gods when the only God is the Almighty – the beginning and the end? In what way are we like him in being self-existent? Are we also now the makers of heaven and earth and owners of everything? In what way are we infinite, unlimited, or unending? For sure, we are not now all-powerful or omnipresent. Nor are we unchanging. This theology of our being gods just doesn't make sense.

If we are little gods what likeness shall we compare to him? Isaiah's exalted vision of God should cause us to bow our heads in shame.

> To whom will you compare me? Or who is my equal? Says the Holy One. Lift up your eyes and look to the heavens: Who created all these? He who brings out the starry host one by one, and calls them each by name. Because of his great power and mighty strength, not one of them is missing.(Isa 40:25–26)

Who are we to liken ourselves to God?

While many external factors may influence or put pressure on us, it is at the individual level that our perceptions of God are established. To really get to know God as he is, we must all deliberately confront the reality of God at the personal level, for that is where we recreate God in our own image or the image of our environment. Rather than imposing our personal understanding on the church or the world, we must subject it to the searchlight of the word of God, the Bible. And even when we listen to Scripture, it must be with an openness to encounter God in all that he is, not in a selective way that will give us a distorted and unbalanced knowledge of him.

Meeting God – Transcendent and Immanent

I would be the last to say I have fully figured God out. Yet in my pilgrimage I have come to appreciate that my old notion of a God of instant justice was a less than true picture of God.

For several years after I became a Christian, my foundational concept of a vengeful God continued to influence my relationship with him. I continually sought to make myself acceptable to him. In my prayer life, the greater portion of my moments before God was spent in preparing myself to enter his presence. My times of multiple repentance were often much longer than those of worship.

My late wife, Tope, introduced me to the God who is both transcendent and immanent; a God whose love for justice does not conflict with his love of the convict. When she approached God, Tope often didn't bother with the rituals of "preparation". She exalted in and exuded the worship of God. As I prayed with her and listened to her pray, I saw her full assurance that Christ has satisfied every ritual or preparation necessary for her and all of us to approach the throne of grace. Whereas I needed at least ten kilometres of prayers to get to the throne of grace, Tope was there within seconds. She needed no long-winded words of repentance; she simply acknowledged Christ's atonement for her on the cross and received God's forgiveness for her shortcomings. She was specific about any and all shortcomings; there were no theological cover-ups. What always amazed me most was her immediate assurance of forgiveness and how easy it was for her to move beyond herself to intercede for others. Her full confidence in God's love and nearness to us lifted me from being permanently at the feet of God to daring to sit on his lap as a child would draw near to his or her father.

Through Tope, I got to understand better that this God who judges all sins is also the one who spoke to Moses face to face as a man to his friend. He was the same God who did not destroy the renegade Jacob in a flash of lightening. I began to read the Old Testament in a new light and discovered that even the Old Testament God was a God at hand. He didn't just throw sinners into wastepaper baskets. He turned Jacob round. He used a prostitute named Rachel and guaranteed her a place in the Promised Land. In giving Nineveh a second chance, he was much more compassionate than the prophet Jonah (who would rather have seen the city destroyed). He was truly a God who is "gracious and compassionate, slow to anger and abounding in love, a God who relents from sending calamity". I began to love this God more and more. I longed to see his face.

In 1980, another friend helped me overcome my preconception that God was a frowning, angry, judgemental deity. A group of five or six of us were seated in a circle in my room in Bauchi State, Northern Nigeria, praying together. We prayed one after the other. Gradually, our prayer became conversational. I do not recall how long we prayed. But I do recall that our prayer soon became pure thanksgiving, interspersed with moments of silence. Then I looked up and saw Uzo, one of us in the circle. She was smiling, then laughing, with a look of complete contentment on her face.

In the long silence that followed, there was no doubt that we all knew God's presence was with us. Afterwards, I told Uzo that I saw her smiling and laughing.

Her response was, "Yes, I saw him, he was there with us … He was also smiling, so happy with us."

"Really?" I asked, "How did you see him?"

"He was on a great white throne, purer than all cloud or light, like the Ancient of Days."

"And he was smiling?"

"Yes," Uzo said calmly.

An "Ancient of Days" who smiles?

Long after the others had gone, I asked Uzo, "Do you always see God this way?"

"No," she replied, "At times he comes to me like Jesus, holding me like a little girl in his hands, walking with me on dusty roads."

"You mean every time you pray you see God in one way or another?"

Uzo replied, "At times I see him and many times I don't, but it doesn't matter whether I see him or not, I know he is with me. There are times I just focus on him and listen to him. He tells me how much he loves the whole world and me; how he desires all to know him."

Uzo talked for a long time, telling me some of her conversations with God.

"Is it only when you pray that you feel so close to God or free to talk with him?" I asked her.

"No! He is always with me. Many times I talk to him when I'm alone in the kitchen or bathroom. I tell him I'm going to the market or to the school. At times I just go somewhere quiet and watch people as they pass. Then I talk to God about them."

Now, I should say that Uzo was neither crazy nor eccentric. She was one of the most ordinary and simple people I have ever come across. Yet her sense of intimacy in her encounters with God was as authentic as her daily display of love towards other people. Through her I came to appreciate both the "otherliness" of God and his identification with us.

Uzo's "Ancient of Days" who smiles made me understand the incarnation much more. I realised that Immanuel, God with us, was not different from the transcendent God of the Hebrews. In and through Immanuel, who ate with sinners, played with little children and travelled dusty roads with so diverse a group as the twelve disciples, we can draw near to God without discrediting his transcendence.

Today, however, our familiarity with God has bred contempt that leads up to trivialise his transcendence. The fact that God cares for us should not lead us to believe that he can be manipulated. I am therefore grateful for my foundational faith, however flawed it may have been, in a God who is just and of purer eyes than to behold iniquity. I am grateful for knowledge of the person of Christ in whom transcendence walked on dusty roads as God with us. This Immanuel clearly demonstrated the lack of conflict between a God of justice and of love. The one who said, "Unless your righteousness surpasses that of the Pharisees and the teachers of the law, you will certainly not enter the kingdom of heaven" (Matt 5:20) is the same one who said to the thief on the cross, "Today you will be with me in paradise" (Luke 23:43). What an awesome God we serve!

Our Response – Worship

How then should we respond to this God; the God who became human without ceasing to be God? The Almighty who stepped into time without leaving eternity! The high and lofty one who inhabits eternity past, present and future! Neither bound by time nor confined by it. Who is like the Lord our God? Majestic in holiness, awesome in glory! These words are not mere repetition. In my culture, the way to acknowledge and give due honour to a person is to publicly declare who they are and all they have done. God deserves no less. Our only response to this God must be worship!

If this is really our God, we each ought to say, as the psalmist said, "What shall I return to the LORD for all his goodness to me? (Ps 116:12).

The catechism used to ask, "What is the chief end of man?" The answer would be, "The chief end of man is to know God and enjoy him forever!" Our purpose is to glorify God and enjoy him for forever. We must begin by seeking to know and understand God (Jer 9:23–24), which will lead us to sincere and spirit-filled worship. Then we must seek to do his will through an obedient life. Our chief purpose is to worship God! Evelyn Underhill in *Worship* says, "Worship is the total adoring response of man to the one Eternal God, self-revealed in time."[7]

A. W. Tozer asks, "Why did Christ come? Why was He conceived? Why was He born? Why was He crucified? Why did He rise again? Why is He now at the right hand of the Father?" His response was, "In order that He might make worshippers out of rebels; in order that He might restore us again to the place of worship we knew when we were first created."[8]

Oh that we would prostrate ourselves before him in worship and declare as David did:

> Yours, Lord, is the greatness and the power
> And the glory and the majesty and the splendour,
> For everything in heaven and earth is yours.
> Yours, Lord, is the kingdom;
> You are exalted as head over all. (1 Chr 29:11)

10

PHONEY CHRISTIANITY

You are the salt of the earth. But if the salt loses its saltiness, how can it be made salty again? It is no longer good for anything, except to be thrown out and trampled underfoot.
— Matthew 5:13

While "modern" preachers and "gospels" of today have much to say about our inheritance in Christ, they say too little about the need for us to be constantly transformed by the renewal of our minds. And while so much is said about our prosperity in the world, not enough is being taught on our calling to be transforming agents in the world.

About twelve years ago I wanted to write a book on how Africa, the continent that was once dark, had seen a great light and been transformed into a continent of light. At the time I was a student at Wheaton Graduate School and was disappointed by what I considered the lukewarm Christianity of Americans. You see, I had grown up captivated by the biographies of men like Billy Sunday, Jonathan Edwards and Charles Finney, whose reviving exploits made an impact on America. I had also been greatly influenced by Mama Kirkpatrick who led me to Christ and whose exemplary life challenged me to forsake all and follow Jesus. I read all I could about the great awakenings and followed closely the ministries of men like Billy Graham, Stephen Olford and Leonard Ravenhill.

When I eventually got to America as a student, I was greatly disappointed by what I saw – the seeming lack of zeal, the prayerlessness and the lack of the aggressive evangelism to which I was accustomed at home. I remember going to church on Christmas Day with Gaius, my roommate, and seeing no one in the auditorium. "These guys don't even go to church on Christmas Day!" That same year I remember telling the editor of *Christianity Today* at the Urbana Conference that Africa no longer needed Western missionaries. Yes, we are grateful for past missionaries, but now we are okay. The church in Africa has grown and we are marching on! The youth are alive and zealous. I dared to tell David Neff and Andres Tapia that America should get ready for African missionaries. "I don't see why missionaries should come to Nigeria from any other country. We've got to reach our own people," I told Andrea Tapia, "We have thousands of Christian graduates, some of whom might have a call but who can't respond because of limited resources." My Jamaican friend, Paulyn Williams chipped in, "We in the Caribbean have been over-evangelised. We are at the point that we need to give or we will stagnate."[1]

Somehow I am yet to write that book, and I am so glad that I have not. How naively sentimental it would have been! After my studies and some time of ministry with InterVarsity Christian Fellowship and at the LaSalle Street Church in Chicago, I returned to the "dark continent" that I said had seen a great light. For the next ten years, I struggled with the tension between the light we had seen and the old darkness that would not go away. Sure, the churches were still full, and the worship was joyful and loud. However, the top leaders had taken more titles and were now Reverend Doctors, Bishops and Apostles. Some drove the latest, most expensive cars, and others would testify that God had blessed them with jets. Although prayer houses, ministries and churches had multiplied across the continent, it was obvious something was missing.

The continuing darkness in Africa has made me wonder if anything has changed. The disintegration of Somalia, the genocide in Rwanda, the ethnic massacres in Burundi and the wars in Liberia and Sierra Leone are all things I would never want to find in history books. It is not that I would expect the light of the gospel to instantly wipe out all human decadence or tragedy in Africa. Yet would it be too much to expect that our light should at least challenge the corrupt image of Lagos, the suffering of the street children of Nairobi, the "cardboard" housing units in Addis Ababa and the thousands of refugees fleeing Liberia, Rwanda and the new but old Democratic Republic of the

Congo? It is as if all our Christian growth and spirituality have been wrapped up and sealed in thick plastic bags so that our light and saltiness have little impact on society. It is amazing how from Sunday to Sunday, wrapped in our thick spiritual plastic bags that have made us immune to societal reality, we continue to say that it is a great thing to serve the Lord.

Crookedness in the Land

There is crookedness on our continent. Only the blind fail to see it. It is very convenient to focus on the crowded churches on Sunday morning and assume there is godliness in the land, but the state of our nations in Africa is lamentable. Our newspapers report this daily, but some of us do not read them because we consider them "secular". But one doesn't have to read the newspapers to know about corruption. We all suffer in one way or other from its effects and from the poor stewardship of resources that has left us dehumanised in many ways. Which African nation has not had its share of leaders who believe more in the politics of the stomach than the politics of accountability? There is dishonour in a land that produces leaders who promise peace and prosperity but inflict poverty and pain, driving people into refugee camps.

From Angola to Zimbabwe, few nations have not known the tragedy of failed leadership. Angola, with some of the world's greatest mineral resources, is a sorry sight. The streets of Luanda are filled with the destitute and the disabled. How can I talk without shame about my own country, Nigeria, when a Nigerian passport is everywhere interpreted as a sign that you are a criminal? Our African leaders include the likes of Idi Amin of Uganda, Samuel Doe of Liberia, Mobutu Sese Seko of Zaire (Democratic Republic of Congo), and Sani Abacha of Nigeria. Those are just a few of the dead. The living still speak for themselves. A leading Western paper once said, "Corruption is so widespread that African leaders no longer disappoint us."

"Western propaganda" we may say, but an African proverb says, "Flies do not herald one who has not polluted the air."

But what has this got to do with the church? "Leave it to the politicians", some would say! "It's their fault. Customs officers are corrupt. The police are no better. The government is responsible for this." It is always easy to blame problems on our leadership. But the reproach of a nation is often a mirror reflecting the face of the church. As a newspaper columnist put it in 1993 during a major national crisis in Nigeria, "There is a Babangida in all of us." At the peak of Nigeria's transition to civil rule in 1993, the military ruler Ibrahim Babangida annulled the election results, bringing the nation close to civil war. There was no end to the attribution of all that happened thereafter to Babangida's greed and self-centredness. He was, of course, responsible, but the "crucify him" cries were often a mask for deeper individual problems.

Should We Not be Concerned?

The truth is, dictators or no dictators, the state of our nation is a reflection of the state of our hearts before God. We have therefore collectively brought reproach on our nations and ourselves. It is not my president who sells rotten tomatoes in the market, hidden under a few brightly coloured ones. It is not just the president who steals government property, even if he sets the example of doing it. It is not only our rulers who are rotten inside. Must we not be concerned that "truth is fallen in the streets"? Should we not be concerned about the increasing population of street children? Should we not be concerned about our young women being exported to Europe as prostitutes? Should we not be concerned about the abuse of our resources by our leaders?

Jeremiah lamented over Jerusalem, "Let us lie down in our shame and our disgrace cover us. We have sinned against the Lord our God" (Jer 3:25). In Lamentations, he cried "Remember, Lord, what has happened to us; look, and see our disgrace" (Lam 5:1). Which of our nations in Africa is not like Jerusalem when "our inheritance has been turned over to strangers, our homes to foreigners. We have become fatherless, our mothers are widows" (Lam 5:2–3).

Jeremiah could be lamenting on behalf of Africa. And while he laments, we continue to play church, happy in our celebrations. Some of us say, "Leave it to the politicians, while we are busy with the affairs of God's house." Could it not be that the reproach of our nations is the reproach of the church and a pointer to our integrity crisis? When the church – the body of Christ – lacks integrity, collectively and individually, the nation cannot but be in reproach. But when the church is alive and walks in the light, it cannot but have an impact in the process of redeeming the nation. When there is fire in the church, society should feel the heat. If there is truly renewal in the church and lives are being transformed, should there not be some signs of a little fruit?

There has been so much talk about the growth of the church in Africa and in other non-Western countries. It has been celebrated in missiological circles. Praise God for this! There is no doubt that the growth of the church in Africa and other parts of the world has significantly changed the identity of the global church. Its former white Western face has become coloured by a new and diverse worldwide heritage. Yet is it not too early to celebrate? How is it that with so much growth, so much evil abounds? It is baffling how our Christian fervour and zeal co-exist with the realities of darkness around us.

I have been in many churches where pastors have to warn women to hold on tightly to their handbags while praying. There are thieves who specialise in snatching handbags on Sunday mornings. They come into churches as neatly dressed as all the others. I have been baffled at how Christian leaders ride in Pajeros in cities where people cannot afford more than one meal a day, and at how churches and ministries accumulate self-serving equipment in situations where people are sleeping on the streets. I've wondered if the gospel has anything to do with the mounds of garbage in the streets of Luanda, Kampala and Dar es Salaam. I have often wondered if the light of our growth has ever had any relationship to the children on the streets of Nairobi, Monrovia or Addis Ababa, where the headquarters of the African Union sits in majestic splendour.

The truth is, within Africa, as in many lands, the church still has a long way to go before it can be a true witness to Christ in society. We still have a long way to go in being light and salt to the continent. Look at Nigeria. New churches and ministries are constantly springing up. I can't think of any other city in the world with as many churches as Lagos. Some streets in Lagos have as many as five church buildings. No week goes by without some significant evangelistic event in Lagos. Yet according to statistical reports, Nigeria has long held the record of being the most corrupt nation in the world. It was only recently that another African country with equally significant church growth records took over the leadership in corruption.

For many years now, Nairobi has been the "Jerusalem" of mission agencies, yet for all its Christian flavour, Nairobi is fast becoming one of the most unsafe cities in Africa. I have witnessed a women being lifted off her feet while in less than fifteen seconds her shoes and jewellery were stolen. It happened too fast for anyone to cry out. Johannesburg is no different. What is needed now is not celebration but heart searching. It is helpful once in a while to withdraw into a closet for individual soul searching. We need to ask, "Am I really in the faith?" "Am I really salt and light in society?"

Where Is the Impact?

Granted, there are communities in which changed lives are having significant influence. There are believers in the marketplace who are refusing to compromise with popular corruption. There are students who are holding fast and living faithfully as witnesses to the cause of Christ. There are simple housewives bearing witness by their honesty and integrity. However, these are very often the exceptions.

Some have argued that we are experiencing problems because the church in Africa is still young, and that with time Christian impact will be felt. But what will happen when we come of age? Will we become like some parts of Europe where former church buildings have been turned into museums or even mosques? When we come of age, do we become like parts of America where the "blessing" of prosperity has allowed materialism to compete with the love of God? It is now, at this point in our growth and renewal, that our society should be being transformed? Do our failures have as much to do with age as with the content of the gospel we are embracing and the lifestyle that results?

I want to suggest two possible reasons why Christians have so little impact on our societies. One is the integrity crisis we have as the church in terms of the gap between our beliefs and practices. The second is that too many of us who know the truth and whose lives have been transformed remain isolated in "church ghettos", wrapped up in our cosy "plastic bags", worshipping and praising the Lord while his world is decaying and remains in darkness. We are like salt that is confined within the salt shaker. But these may merely be symptoms of a much worse malady: a phoney "gospel" that we have imbibed, which has resulted in phoney Christianity.

Christianity Without Integrity

We have an integrity crisis from Nigeria to Namibia, Morocco to Mozambique, Tunisia to Tanzania, simply because our lifestyles do not match our beliefs. It is easy to confess that, "The people walking in darkness have seen a great light; on those living in the land of the deep darkness a light has dawned" (Isa 9:2). Yet we all know only too well that the darkness still competes with the light because too many of us are still crooked in our ways. We are not straight! If the church, which is supposed to be the light of the world, is in darkness, how great is the darkness of the world!

Sadly, this lack of integrity causes God's name to be blasphemed among unbelievers. The world clearly sees the lack of integrity in the church. The following are real incidents involving people who profess to be Christians. All were reported with gusto in African newspapers: a) A regular churchgoer was arrested on his wedding day for having embezzled a very large amount of money from the government department where he worked. b) A Christian "brother" got engaged to two different "sisters" who lived in different cities. He was committed to marrying them both on different days. The invitations to both weddings had already been sent out when his crookedness was revealed.

Then there is Johnson (not his real name), a prominent member of a local chapter of the Full Gospel Businessmen's Fellowship. He is always exuberant and cheerful. He is the liveliest participant when it is time to dance and praise the Lord. He is so visible during offering time that it is hardly a secret what he gives to the Lord. Ask Johnson about his business and his typical response is, "Business is good all the time. The Lord is blessing us, Hal-le-lu-ia!" Yet in the market where Johnson has his store, his reputation is different. Everyone knows he sells substandard goods at standard prices. He cuts corners to make profits and occasionally lies to cover up unpaid taxes and utility bills. The Johnson in the market is utterly different from the Johnson of the Full Gospel Businessmen's Fellowship.

Many others who fill churches from week to week listen to the word and probably have Christian convictions, but do not let these affect their lifestyle.

When those who are supposed to be the light are so dishonest in basic matters, the church may increase in number but it cannot bear witness to the gospel.

There is even dishonesty within the church, not least among its leaders. One hears of pastors making off with a congregation's collection on the pretext that the Bible says all tithes and offerings belong to the priests. There are evangelists who write to Western donors to report fake success stories in order to bring in more funds.

One such case was referred to me by a group in the United States. Someone had appealed to them for funds for his ministry and for an orphanage he was running. I was requested to verify the information he provided. Armed with the address of the ministry and orphanage, my wife and I travelled to the city where it was supposed to be located. After extensive search and inquiries, we discovered that the ministry and the orphanage did not exist!

Another time, someone sent photographs of his ministry centre and outreach points to accompany a request for funds. But it was discovered that he had no connection to the property shown in the photos. Pressed to explain this discrepancy, he said the photographs showed his vision for the ministry he hoped to have. He was exercising faith! The photographs were his "substance of things hoped for, the evidence of things not seen". It is amazing how God's word can be twisted!

Christianity Without Impact

The story of "Sister" illustrates Christianity without impact. Everyone called her "Sister" in the corporate office where she worked. Perhaps it was because she wore a large "Jesus Saves" badge on her blouse. Or because she never started her day in the office without praying loudly in tongues, something which was not lost on her mostly non-Christian colleagues. After praying, Sister would dig in her handbag for her Bible, which she would read while others worked. Sister did not socialise with anyone in the office; she would sometimes not even respond to a greeting. Her intense frown was enough to discourage anyone trying to be friendly. Her colleagues did not like her because she was lazy with her work and never on time with assignments. When her boss queried her preparing Bible study materials during office hours, she reported to friends that she was being persecuted for the sake of the gospel. When one saw Sister leading praise and worship at fellowship group and smiling at everyone, it was difficult to imagine that she was the same person who did not relate to anyone in her workplace.

I know of a Christian guesthouse that is surrounded by piles of refuse. I have watched as people from the guesthouse and others from the street throw more refuse onto the mound. The stench filtered through the windows into the rooms. I ventured to ask whose responsibility it was to clear the refuse. I was told it was the government's responsibility, but that they had not come for a long time. I looked around me and discovered many mounds of refuse on the streets, some very near doorsteps. Most citizens were simply waiting for government to do something. Meanwhile, they continued to heap the refuse higher and higher.

One sees the same lack of initiative or creativity to transform the environment in government offices, where clerks say, "It's a government job, why should I kill myself doing it?" There are Christians who live in government housing units who neglect to do basic maintenance, simply because it is not their property. Such an attitude is anything but biblical.

This attitude is fuelled by our tendency to draw too sharp a distinction between what is sacred and what is secular, or between what we consider spiritual and what we consider earthly. We assume that clearing refuse, maintaining the environment and good stewardship of government resources are "secular" commitments, and so we don't bother with them. We confine our lives and commitments to the things we consider sacred or spiritual.

This attitude also makes us think that some people are called to full-time Christian ministry while the rest of us are not in ministry; we are just working. Such thinking accounts for much of the apathy, job dissatisfaction and mediocrity among Christians in the so-called secular professions. We need to return to a biblical perspective which considers all of life as sacred. For Christians, all work or professional commitments should be full-time ministry.

Christianity Without Walls

There is an urgent need to break the walls of church-ianity and instead reflect on true Christianity. There is a desperate need for integration, for the involvement of Christians with the challenges of the marketplace. We must take seriously the need to apply our faith and biblical values to the darkness of our land. We must come to terms with the fact that the state of our nations must not be left to politicians alone to decide. We must not allow the blind to lead the blind.

This is not to suggest that being a Christian automatically imbues one with the skills of good governance or the management of societal resources. It is, however, a blessing when those who profess to know God combine their service to him with the essential skills of management. Christian intellectuals who are in government must not abdicate the formulation of policy to men who are still in darkness.

It has been rightly observed that many of the tragedies in Africa are not accidental. They are direct results of deliberate government policies. Hugh McCullum believes this was the case in Rwanda during the 1994 genocide. In *The Angels Have Left Us,* his account of the tragedy and the churches' involvement, McCullum writes:

> The massacres inside Rwanda and what happened outside in the camps were not accidents of war, in which civilians get caught in the crossfire – horrific and unacceptable in a world we had hoped was becoming more humane, but still a circumstance of war. The massive exodus of refugees swarming into Tanzania, Zaire and to some extent Burundi was not just the upheaval of a people fleeing for their lives, which we have become all too accustomed to seeing on television. It was policy. The killings and the refugee crisis were planned. Whether people survived murderous militias in church compounds or disease and hunger in squalid refugee camps, they were human pawns in a deadly political game whose goal was, and still is, the retention

of power by extremists bent on shaping Rwanda to suit their own twisted ideology.[2]

Sadly, while Christian intellectuals remain silent, our leaders pursue the politics of the stomach and sell out their own people to foreign powers in the name of obtaining foreign aid. Our need of the hour is to respond to the challenge. We need to heed George Kinoti's call:

> The challenge is for African Christians to become active at every level of the development process – from the development of economic and political theory to the formulation and implementation of policy, and from the highest levels of government to the village. Christians must actively participate in the governance of their nations. That is a tremendous challenge, and one which we are not at liberty to evade.[3]

There is such an urgent need for us to get out of plastic bags and be shaken out of the salt shaker. Our Christian convictions are not meant to be sealed up in church and fellowship meetings. They are to influence every decision and action in the public arena and marketplace. The call to have clean hands does not mean that God will not call us to clear refuse heaps or clean up slums.

Many years ago, I was at a conference where most of us were students. We were excited about the fellowship we were enjoying, the praise sessions were excellent and we all felt spirit-filled. The Bible exposition was top-notch and deep. One afternoon, the leader asked for volunteers to help clean the bathrooms, which were messy and foul-smelling. They were not a place where anyone wanted to stay too long. The same announcement was repeated the following day, indicating that no one had yet volunteered. Again no one volunteered; we were too excited about getting filled. "Spiritual" students shouldn't clean bathrooms, should they? Then we noticed that the bathrooms began to get neater. We tried to find out who was cleaning them, but couldn't until the last day of the conference. It turned out that a Ghanaian brother had been secretly going into the bathrooms with a broom and a bucket each night after others were asleep. Asked why he did it, he simply said that he had the gift of "helping". While many of us were too busy with the utterance gifts of tongues and prophecy, this brother was cleaning toilets that no one else would clean. That brother translated his convictions into practice.

In 1997 I met another group of students who refused to be plastic bag Christians. I had a one-day stopover in Libreville, Gabon, and contacted Scott and Mishael Harris, who were on staff with IFES in Gabon. They invited me over to the university campus where Christian students were welcoming new students. They had begun by cleaning the bathrooms and fixing the doorknobs on campus. They had approached the Students Affairs office for new door handles and other resources they needed, but they did the cleaning up themselves. Then as the new students arrived, they welcomed them with smiles, took their luggage and helped them to settle into their rooms. The goal that day was not to preach to the new students; it was to give them the best possible welcome to a clean environment and to build relationships.

As I interacted with these students, I knew there was hope for Africa. We need many more such happenings across our land. This is what involvement is. And it should extend beyond the campus to our communities and nations. We must translate Christian convictions and values into day-to-day practice. We must restore the dignity of our land and re-affirm over and over again that because this is God's world, we must be involved. We can begin to do this only when we reject self-centred gospels that seek to keep us in our comfort zones.

11

AUTHENTIC CHRISTIANITY

The authentic Christianity of the Bible is not a safe, smug, cosy, selfish, little religion. On the contrary, it is an explosive, centrifugal force, which pulls us out from our narrow self-centredness and flings us into God's world to witness and to serve.
— John Stott

The problem with anything that is phoney is that it appears to be true. But appearance should not be the basis for determining authenticity. Jesus warned his disciples not to try to distinguish the true from the false by mere appearance.

"Watch out for false prophets," Jesus said, "They come to you in sheep's clothing, but inwardly they are ferocious wolves" (Matt 7:15). His counsel to the disciples, and therefore also to us today, is to look at the fruit of their lives.

> By their fruit you will recognize them. Do people pick grapes from thornbushes, or figs from thistles? Likewise every good tree bears good fruit, but a bad tree bears bad fruit. A good tree cannot bear bad fruit, and a bad tree cannot bear good fruit. Every tree that does not bear good fruit is cut down and thrown into the fire. Thus, by their fruit you will recognise them. (Matt 7:16–20)

The problem with fruit is that it does not appear immediately. It takes time. This means that we cannot determine whether a teacher is true or false on the basis of just one incident or meeting. The quality of the teacher's life and the consistency of his or her teaching with biblical revelation are what authenticate them as truly Christian.

We must therefore search the Scriptures for ourselves and watch our lives and those of our teachers closely. The best way to avoid being misled from the truth or purpose of the gospel is to be grounded in the knowledge of the Bible. We must be grounded in the truth, associate with those who are committed to the gospel of Christ, and seek to bring that gospel to bear on every aspect of our lives as individuals and as the community of God's people.

Grounded in Scripture

Some of us are content to rely on pastors or other "experts" to give us an understanding of the word of God rather than studying the Bible ourselves. Others prefer to live only on the "word of prophecy" or "new revelations" of other people rather than develop the discipline of daily Bible study and obedience. It is so easy to be misled if we are unwilling to use our God-given minds to study and think through the word of God, especially since those who preach and teach false gospels also read the Bible and claim to speak for God. Some of those who teach false gospels use their personal experiences as the basis for truth, forgetting that truth must be the basis of experience and not the other way round.

> All Scripture is God-breathed and is useful for teaching, rebuking, correcting and training in righteousness, so that all God's people may be thoroughly equipped for every good work. (2 Tim 3:16)

Thus we need to devote ourselves to studying all Scripture, and not to be content with just hearing what others have to say to us about it. Yes, we need to hear it expounded by teachers, but we also need to study it individually and in small groups, allowing our minds to grasp its truth.

If we all read the same Bible, why are there so many "gospels"? The answer lies in how we interpret the Bible. Some claim to have an anointing that entitles them to some divine interpretation that is beyond the rest of us. They urge us to listen to them and follow what they say as though it were equivalent to what the Apostles taught. Others interpret the Scriptures without recognising that the Bible contains different types of literature or genres, including prophecies, narratives and historical texts, prose and poetry, metaphors, hyperbole and similes, and didactic or expositional texts. We need to read and interpret the Bible in a way that does not distort its message.

In reading the Bible, our goal must be to seek what God intends us to know and understand from the text, not what *we* intend to find. The primary objective is to read "out of" the text the meaning of the author – both the human and divine author – as it was understood by the audience for whom it was originally intended and then apply it ourselves in our times. The Holy Spirit who inspired the authors of the different books will illuminate the word to us. No Christian or teacher has more of the Holy Spirit than other Christians. We should therefore not be intimidated by any claims to special "inspiration", words of knowledge or words of prophecy.

One of the most important factors to take into consideration is that the different genres in the Bible are rooted in different historical-cultural contexts. In interpreting any biblical text, it is important that we consider both its literary and historical-cultural context. For example, the Psalms, which are written in a poetic style, have to be interpreted in a different way from the gospels, which are narratives. In interpreting prophetic passages, we need to determine the context the prophecy is given, its distant but contextual fulfilment, and how it fits into the Christ-event – the fact that the Messiah has come and will return as judge. We cannot read the Old Testament, which looks to the coming of the Messiah, the same way we read the New Testament, which was written after the Messiah was revealed. We must always remember that each text was born in a particular culture and time.

We are privileged to live at a time when there are many study tools available to help us. It is good to make use of them. First of all, find a good translation of the Bible. The sixty-six books of the Bible were originally written in three different languages: Hebrew, Greek and Aramaic. The versions we use today are all translations. It helps to have a good translation, and compare several translations and versions. An annotated Bible – with notes, footnotes and cross-references – is even more helpful.

Secondly, select a good Bible commentary. There are different types: exegetical commentaries focus on the original words; historical commentaries on the original context; theological commentaries on the doctrinal implications of a text; homiletical commentaries on the use of a text in preaching; and devotional commentaries on spiritual nourishment.

Thirdly, there are other tools such as Bible concordances to help identify cross-references; Bible dictionaries, which give background information; and Bible atlases that give you a bit more about the geographical settings in which the events recorded in the Bible occurred.

The importance of studying the Scriptures and "rightly handling the word of truth" cannot be overemphasised. Jesus warned very clearly that prior to his return, there would be many false prophets, including some claiming to be the Christ, who would distort the truth. He said in Matthew 24:5:

> Watch out that no one deceives you. For many will come in my name claiming, "I am the Messiah", and will deceive many.

He also warned that,

> At that time many will turn away from the faith and will betray and hate each other, and many false prophets will appear and deceive many people. (Matt 24:10–11)

This is already very much with us. False teachers and prophets use diverse ways to deceive many. What may look very attractive or popular to us may be detestable to God.

Jesus warned in another passage that we must not assume that anyone who claims to have the ability to work miracles necessarily does so to the praise of God:

> Not everyone who says to me, "Lord, Lord" will enter the kingdom of heaven, but only those who do the will of my Father who is in heaven. Many will say to me on that day, "Lord, Lord, did we not prophecy in your name and in your name drive out demons and in your name perform many miracles?" Then I will tell them plainly, "I never knew you. Away from me, you evildoers!" (Matt 7:21–23)

A clear principle we learn from this is that miracles do not authenticate a minister of the gospel. We must examine the quality and content of a person's life and teaching in the light of the revealed will of God in the Bible.

The Apostles also wrote to warn believers not to follow teachers who were presenting gospels different from what they had taught. Paul warned that not only would the number of such teachers increase in the last days, but that some of their teachings would be energised by demons (1 Tim 4:1). In his letters, Peter indicated that false teachers would introduce their destructive heresies in subtle ways (2 Pet 2:1). He warned that they would seek to exploit the church (2:3) and take delight in pleasures (2:13). In addition to their being experts in greed (2:14), they would forsake the right way (2:15).

If we do not resist such teachers and their doctrines, however appealing they may be, the ultimate risk is that we, too, may drift from the right way and embrace a different gospel, which is really no gospel at all (Gal 1:6–7). The way to resist them is by understanding the truth ourselves.

Committed to the Gospel

This is why it is really important for us to know and commit ourselves to the true gospel. We must not follow all kinds of false teachings that complicate or contradict the gospel of our Lord Jesus Christ. Concerning the gospel, Paul writes:

> I am not ashamed of the gospel, because it is the power of God that brings salvation to everyone who believes; first to the Jew, then to the Gentile. For in the gospel the righteousness of God is revealed – a righteousness that is by faith from first to last, just as it is written: "The righteous will live by faith".
> (Rom 1:16–17)

The gospel of Christ is the good news of God's love for us and his desire that we live in peace with him eternally. It is the good news that peace with God comes through Jesus Christ alone (Rom 5:1).

The primary reason Jesus came into the world was so that "whoever believes in him shall not perish but have eternal life" (John 3:16). The benefits of the gospel are primarily eternal, and are not just here and now in this life.

Christ had to come because sin had separated all of humanity from the eternal God. Like Adam who fell into sin from the very beginning, we all often choose to disobey God. The Bible says, "For all have sinned and fall short of the glory of God" and reminds us that "the wages of sin is death" (Rom 3:23; 6:23). It is not too popular today to point out to people that they have sinned and are therefore separated from God. However, any gospel that downplays human sinfulness and the eternal benefits of the gospel is not a gospel of Christ. If we were not separated from God by our sins, we would not have needed a saviour. This is essentially why Christ came, to save us from our sins (Matt 1:21), that we may inherit eternal life. He did this by dying on the cross. "God demonstrated his own love for us in this: while we were still sinners, Christ died for us" (Rom 5:8). This is why only Jesus can boldly declare, "I am the way and the truth and the life. No one comes to the Father except through me" (John 14:6).

Any preaching of the gospel that denigrates the cross of Christ is not true to biblical revelation. This was so important to Paul that he had to write the following words to the church at Corinth:

> When I came to you, I did not come with eloquence or human wisdom as I proclaimed to you the testimony about God. For I resolved to know nothing while I was with you except Jesus Christ and him crucified. (1 Cor 2:1–2)

Beyond understanding the gospel, we should bear in mind the purpose for which it was delivered to us. Was it just so that we could have a good time and be materially prosperous? Was it just to give us a secret key to anything we desire? Definitely not. While there is room for excitement about God's gift of salvation to us, we must not forget that the primary purpose of the gospel is to save us and bring us into a living relationship with God and with one another. The goal is to produce transformed people who bear witness to the righteousness of God.

God expects us to respond to the claims of Jesus by believing in him and receiving his gift of salvation. It is only in this way that we can experience God's forgiveness, his peace and righteousness. "To all who did receive him, to those who believed in his name, he gave the right to become children of God (John 1:12).

The gospel is therefore the power of God to save anyone who will call on him. Anyone who recognises that he is a sinner and is willing to turn away from his sins, and who believes that Jesus Christ died on the cross and rose from the grave for the purpose of saving him, can through a simple prayer become a child of God.

In short, Jesus is the gospel. The gospel is simple and straightforward enough for us to be able to avoid those who complicate it by adding something of their own to distort it. Any gospel that distorts the person or mission of Jesus Christ is no gospel at all. Any gospel that emphasises miracles or prosperity above Christ's death and resurrection is suspect. And any preacher or teacher who exalts himself or herself above Christ and his mission is no messenger of God at all.

The Church – Transforming Society

The gospel created the church. The church is not just a physical building or a group of people who follow some rules and give regular offerings. The church is God's new society in the world – a people transformed by the gospel, proclaiming the gospel and sharing it with a world in darkness. The church is a community of people who have turned their lives over to Christ and now live according to his standards; of people whose faith and conduct demonstrate the values of the kingdom of God. In other words, members of this community believe and are committed to practising the righteousness of God. It is for this reason that Paul says:

> His intent was that now, through the church, the manifold wisdom of God should be made known to the rulers and authorities in the heavenly realms, according to his eternal purpose that he accomplished in Christ Jesus our Lord. (Eph 3:10–11)

The chief goal of the church is not just to have a good time or to be materially prosperous. We are called to be witnesses to God's salvation plan for humanity. We are called to be transforming agents as light and salt in society. The gospel that creates the church also transforms communities and societies in which the church is, through the church.

The impact of our salvation experience is not meant to be confined within the physical walls of a church building. We are called to a holistic mission that seeks to transform the kingdoms of this world into the kingdom of our God. One of our greatest needs today is to return to the true gospel of Christ, which has power to radically affect character and make us all that God really wants us to be. When the gospel transforms one's character the benefit is that through us, that is, the church, the larger society is influenced for the better.

Various communities of God's renewed people have always had ways of influencing their immediate world with kingdom values. That was the pattern with the early church. They were not only different from other people in their beliefs and practices but engaged their world from day to day. Their impact was such that they were once accused of having "turned the world upside down" (Acts 17:6, KJV). Biblical truth, as expressed in the life of the church, should impact our societies in such ways that people's world views and lifestyles continue to be changed to conform more and more to God's standards. The only way to do this is for each of us who names the name of Christ and identifies with him to stand firm and be faithful to the true gospel that has been entrusted to the saints. For the gospel to impact our nations with kingdom values, we must, as people who profess to be Christian, ask ourselves if we are really different from those who make no such claim. This difference must be apparent not just in our convictions or confessions, but much more importantly in our day-to-day conduct. I must ask myself whether my life indicates that I am walking in the light of the gospel. If I claim to follow Jesus, does my life reflect his?

This is very important for us Christians to consider because in all honesty there are many of us who claim to follow him and yet have very little to show for it. Our lives are so different from his. While we have knowledge of his words, our lives do not reflect the essence of his teachings. If Jesus is the truth, and in him there is no deceit, why do we who claim to follow him live double lives – in words and deeds, in pretexts and exaggerations? Why does our Christ-likeness melt when it comes to matters of honesty, our use of money, and so forth? As a university student, the question that baffled me most then (and still baffles me to some extent today) is, "If I truly know and love Jesus, why am I so different from him?" The answer, I realised, it that it is not so much knowing God that matters but following him in all obedience.

Need for Integrity

The *Collins English Dictionary* defines integrity as "adherence to moral principles; honesty, the quality of being unimpaired; soundness, wholeness." The word comes from the Latin word "integritas", which means "wholeness", "entireness", or "completeness". The root is "integer", which means "untouched", "intact", "entire". Christians are meant to be people of integrity. They are meant to be whole and not divided. They are meant to be complete and not impaired, single-minded and not pretentious. In belief and practice they are meant to be sound. In conduct, because they are in Christ, they are to be straightforward and not crooked.

The cross is a good symbol to illustrate integrity. The cross consists of two straight lines, one vertical and the other horizontal. The vertical line can be used to illustrate God's love reaching down to us and the horizontal line to illustrate our interpersonal relationship with one another. When we are as straight as these two lines in our relationship with God and with one another, we are laying a foundation for integrity. Without the cross and all that it represents, there can be no true integrity. The lines that symbolise the cross are not crooked but straight. Integrity is about being straight with God and others. When one is not straight or right with God, one cannot be straight with people.

We have examples of people who were not too straight in Scripture. The story of Ananias and Sapphira (Acts 5:1–11) comes to mind. Joseph, who was also called Barnabas (which means "son of encouragement"), had sold a field he owned and brought the proceeds to the Apostles. The Bible doesn't say whether Barnabas was praised or not, but Ananias and Sapphira decided to do the same. They also sold a piece of property and brought part of the proceeds to the Apostles. However, they gave the impression that they had brought *all* the proceeds. They probably wanted to impress the Apostles and stand before the church as equal to Barnabas in faith and generosity. They wanted some credit or praise, but deliberately planned how to obtain it without paying the price.

They lacked the "whole-heartedness" or "integrity" of Barnabas. Their desire for recognition or approval without a clean heart made them resort to deceit. So they made a false appearance. They had the right to keep *all* the money! They were not under pressure to sell the land or give part or all of it. Their sin was not keeping part of the proceeds from their sale but pretending that they were handing *all* of it over. This was hypocrisy. Their deceit progressed to lies, not just to people but God.

We read of the consequences of their lack of integrity. Just as they were united in deceit, Ananias and Sapphira were united in judgement. The discipline they received was severe because it was meant to serve as an example to the early church. It reveals God's displeasure with sin, and particularly with dishonesty in the church. There is much for us to learn from this story, even if it is not common for people to be struck dead for such sins these days.

We must be people of integrity whatever the cost. I know a leader who refused to compromise his integrity when interviewed by a donor agency. He was the general secretary of one of our student movements. A representative of the agency had come to interview him because they were interested in his movement's ministry. The visitor explained that his agency was particularly interested in helping the poor and asked the leader, "Do you work with the poor?" This brother could have answered, "Yes, most students are poor", but instead he answered honestly, "No not specifically with the poor but with the leaders of tomorrow." That was the end of the interview. He did not get the funds but he did maintain his integrity. We need many more Christians like that, people who stick to the truth because Jesus is the truth. This is what integrity is all about.

Impact in Society

True renewal is not just personal; it must also have an impact on society. The Welsh revivals, the great American Awakenings of the nineteenth century and the East African Revival that broke out in the early 1930s bear testimony to this. All the accounts of them record their impact in their immediate context at that time.

Authentic Christianity 139

One dimension of this impact relates to the role of leadership. Highlighting the need for sound leadership in the church in Africa, George Kinoti says:

> I am aware of the rapid growth of the African church. But this growth is largely numerical. The church is, I suggest, without a strong biblical or theological foundation of her own. I fear that this rapid growth may prove to be like the growth of the seed in a thin layer of soil that soon withers for lack of nourishment. The church requires large numbers of well-educated, spiritually minded pastors who are able to serve all social classes. We need high quality theological colleges, which will train pastors, carry out research and develop theologies that are truly biblical and relevant to the African political, economic and social realities.[1]

Recently, I was at a conference of young people in Khartoum, Sudan. There were about 350 present and it was obvious God was at work. Many of them turned their lives over to Christ and others made commitments to be his witnesses. All this was in an environment of hostile Islamic repression. In the interactive session that followed my seminar, a Westerner stood up to ask a question. He asked, "The churches in Africa are growing rapidly ... I consider this the same as other continents which received Christianity before Africa and which now are not as active as Africa. Can we consider that soon Africa will resemble these continents, or is there something special in the growth of its churches?"

That was an important question with serious implications. I thought very deeply before answering him. There is no doubt that historically the Great Awakenings in Europe and America had a significant impact on society in their time. Jails were emptied, crime decreased and society at large became affected by Christian values. It is also true that these continents which experienced God's visitation in the past now appear to have slid back.

Church history records great revivals in Britain, including the Welsh Revival and the revival under John Wesley. But today Britain clearly seems to have lost it. While there is still a dynamic remnant or a new beginning of revival, the older churches that were part of the earlier revivals have become empty. Many are no more than relics; some have become mosques.

There were also the great revivals in North America under men like Charles Finney, Jonathan Edwards and others. Yet secularism, pluralism and other influences now compete with the Christian values that once shaped America. It is so sad that many of the nations that were touched by these revivals are not continuing in the newness of life brought into their lives. It is sad that many places in which the Apostle Paul and others once planted churches have been overtaken by Islam or have only relics of ancient churches to show for their labours in Christ.

It would be foolish of us to assume that the same cannot happen in Africa. The genocide in Rwanda should be a warning to us. The East African Revival started in Uganda and spread to Rwanda and transformed many lives. The flames of the revival spread all over East Africa, producing faithful men and women who walked in the light. Yet, less than a half-century later, Rwanda exploded with ethnic intolerance and violence. What had become of the revival?

No one should pretend that there are easy answers to the questions raised by the Rwandan tragedy. Nevertheless we must learn lessons from it. We must know that rapid church growth or expansion is no guarantee that all human frailties and depravity are automatically dealt with. We must not assume that all converts are necessarily disciples. Nor must we think we stand on a higher moral pedestal and are exempt from the challenges of such situations.

This raises a challenge for the present rapid growth of the church in Africa. We must be careful to guard the gospel jealously so as not to experience the same kind of decline. It is important to look back at the rich heritage of the church that has been passed on to us. From that rich heritage and faithfulness to the Bible, Africa can strive towards a Christian legacy that will stand the test of time. From ancient North Africa we have the rich heritage of Augustine, Bishop of Hippo, who emphasised the grace of God for salvation and life. The Germans gave us Martin Luther who emphasised justification by faith. The English Puritans and their American successors gave us a legacy of holiness and hard work. From the East African Revival, which emphasised walking in the light, we can recommit ourselves to transparency. With so rich a heritage, why should we drift from such a solid foundation to embrace shallow and trivial counterfeit gospels that focus more on earthly pleasures and freedom from temporary inconveniences?

Above all, in place of the various gospels of our days, we must return to the gospel as it was once delivered to the saints. It alone is the power of God unto salvation. In it alone can we recover the simplicity of Christ, which is fast fading from the church. To embrace this gospel is to encounter the person of Christ as Saviour and Lord. The result is a lifestyle that reflects the life of Christ and that seeks to impact others with kingdom values. The words of Paul to Timothy should continue to be our watchword today.

> Watch your life and doctrine closely. Persevere in them, because if you do, you will save both yourself and your hearers. (1 Tim 4:16)

NOTES

Chapter 2. Strange Times, Strange Gospel

1 Warren W. Wiersbe, *The Integrity Crisis* (Nashville; Oliver Nelson Books, 1988), 17.

2 Oswald Chambers, *My Utmost for His Highest* (London: Marshall, Morgan & Scott, 1972), 241.

Chapter 3. Between the Cross and Champagne

1 As told by Derek Joy in an unpublished paper on the Gindiri revival.

2 First stanza of "It's not an easy road" by John W. Peterson.

3 David Oyedepo, *Breaking Financial Hardship* (Lagos: Dominion Publishing House, 1995), 53.

4 Ibid., 57.

5 A. W. Tozer, *The Divine Conquest* (Camp Hill, Pennsylvania: Christian Publications, 1950), 59.

6 A. W. Tozer, *The Root of the Righteous* (Camp Hill, Pennsylvania: Christian Publications, 1955), 61.

7 Ibid., 66.

8 Dietrich Bonhoeffer, *The Cost of Discipleship* (London: SCM, 2001), 33.

Chapter 4. Charismatic Renewal and Confusion

1 Samuel Escobar, *A Time for Mission: The Challenge for Global Christianity* (Leicester: IVP, 2003), 114.

2 Walter J. Hollenweger, *Pentecostalism: Origins and Developments Worldwide* (Peabody, Mass.: Hendrickson, 1997), 20.

3 David Oyedepo, *The Release of Power* (Lagos: Dominion Publishing House, 1996), 126–127.

4 A. W. Tozer, *The Divine Conquest* (Camp Hill, Penn: Christian Publications, 1950), 47.

Chapter 5. The "Modern" Preachers

1 Warren W. Wiersbe, *The Integrity Crisis* (Nashville, Tenn: Oliver-Nelson Books, 1988), 46–47.

2 Ibid., 69.

Chapter 6. Misreading the Scriptures

1 Robert Tilton, *God's Miracle Plan for Man* (Dallas: Robert Tilton Ministries, 1987), 36.
2 See William Macdonald, *Believer's Bible Commentary* (Nashville: Thomas Nelson, 1980), 143.
3 David O. Oyedepo, *Covenant Wealth* (Lagos: Dominion Publishing House, 1992), 3.
4 Ibid., 4.
5 Jim Bakker in an interview with *Charisma* (February 1997), 48–49.
6 Ibid., 48.
7 Earl Paulk, *Satan Unmasked* (Atlanta: K. Dimension Publishers, 1984), 97.
8 John Avanzini with Morris Cerullo, *The End Time Manifestations of the Sons of God* (San Diego: Morris Cerullo World Evangelism, n.d.) Audiotape, side 1. Quoted in Hank Hanegraaff, *Christianity in Crisis* (Milton Keynes, England: Nelson Word, 1995), 108–109.
9 Ibid., Audiotapes 1, sides 1 & 2.
10 Casey Treat, "Believing in Yourself", tape 2 in a four-tape series, as quoted in Dave Hunt and T. A. McMahon, *The Seduction of Christianity* (Eugene, Ore: Christian Life Publishers, 1986), 82–83.
11 Kenneth Copeland, *Word of Faith* (Fort Worth, Tex: Kenneth Copeland, 1980), 14.
12 Kenneth Copeland, "The Force of Love", audiotape #02-0028 (Fort Worth, Tex.: Kenneth Copeland, 1987). On file with the Christian Research Institute (CRI), as quoted in Michael Horton (ed.), *The Agony of Deceit* (Chicago: Moody, 1990), 92.
13 Paul Crouch, "Praise the Lord", Trinity Broadcasting Network, July 7, 1986.
14 The New American Standard Bible uses "rulers" in Psalm 82:1, "gods" in 82:6 and "gods" in Psalm 58:1. The New International Version uses "gods" in Psalm 82:1, "gods" in 82:6 and "rulers" in Psalm 58:1; The Amplified Bible uses "magistrates" and "judges" in Psalm 82:1, "God's representatives" in 82:6 and "mighty men/politicians" in Psalm 58:1.
15 Hank Hanegraaff, *Christianity in Crisis* (Milton Keynes, England: Nelson Word, 1995), 107, quoting M. Scott Peck, *The Road Less Travelled* (New York: Simon & Schuster, 1978), 270.
16 Ibid., 108.

Chapter 7. Counterfeit Faith

1 Kenneth Hagin, *Having Faith in Your Faith* (Tulsa, Okla..: Faith Library, 1980), 4–5.
2 Ibid., 14.
3 Kenneth Copeland, *The Force of Faith* (Fort Worth, Tex: Kenneth Copeland Publication, 1989), 10.

4 Charles Capps, *Authority in Three Worlds* (Tulsa, Okla.: Harrison House, 1982), 24.

5 E. W. Kenyon, *The Hidden Man: An Unveiling of the Subconscious Mind* (Seattle: Kenyon's Gospel Publishing Society, 1969), 99.

6 Kenneth Copeland, "Inner Image of the Covenant" (Fort Worth, Tex: Kenneth Copeland Ministries, 1985) Audiotape #01–4406, side 2, as quoted in Hank Hanegraaff's *Christianity in Crisis*, 81.

7 Kenneth Hagin, *How to Write Your Own Ticket with God* (Tulsa: Faith Library, 1980), 6–8, 11–20, 21, 32.

8 Ibid., 5.

9 Ibid., 6.

10 E. W. Kenyon, *The Two Kinds of Faith: Faith's Secrets Revealed* (Seattle: Kenyon's Gospel Publishing Society, 1942), 67.

11 Charles Capps, *Dynamics of Faith and Confession* (Tulsa, Okla.: Harrison House, 1987), 86–87.

12 Marilyn Hickey Ministries, direct mail place (n.d.) [ca.1992] – as quoted by Hank Hanegraaff in *Christianity in Crisis* (Milton Keynes, England: Nelson Word, 1995), 351.

13 Kenneth Copeland, *The Force of Faith*, 10, 16.

14 Charles Capps, *Can Your Faith Fail?* (Tulsa, Okla.: Harrison House, 1976) pp. 27–28.

15 Charles Capps, *The Tongue: A Creative Force* (Tulsa, Okla: Harrison House, 1976), 92.

16 Kenneth Copeland, presentation at Melodyland Christian Centre, Anaheim, Calif. (30 March 1983) as quoted by Hank Hanegraaff in *Christianity in Crisis*, 263.

17 David O. Oyedepo, *The Law of Faith* (Kaduna: Faith Liberation Hour Ministries, 1985), 18.

18 Kenneth Copeland, *Freedom from Fear* (Fort Worth, Tex: Kenneth Copeland Ministries, 1980), 11–12.

19 David Oyedepo, *Breaking Financial Hardship* (Lagos; Dominion Publishing House, 1995), 131.

20 Dan McConnell, *The Promise of Health and Wealth* (London; Hodder and Stoughton, 1990), 81.

21 See Dave Hunt & T. A. McMahon, *The Seduction of Christianity* (Eugene, Ore. Harvest House, 1985).

22 Dan McConnell, *The Promise of Health and Wealth*, 94.

23 Ibid.

24 Ibid., 13.

Chapter 8. The Delusions of Prosperity

1 Dan McConnell, *The Promise of Health and Wealth* (London; Hodder and Stoughton, 1990), 183.

2 Warren W. Wiersbe, *The Integrity Crisis* (Nashville; Oliver Nelson, 1988), 52.

3 Gordon Fee, "The Cult of Prosperity", 13 as quoted in McConnell's *The Promise of Health and Wealth*, 170.

4 Stephen D. Eyre, *Defeating the Dragons of the World: Resisting the Seduction of False Values* (Downers Grove, Ill.: IVP, 1987), 28.

5 Ibid., 12.

6 Bob Goudzwaard, *Idols of our Time* (Downers Grove, Ill:. IVP, 1984), 13.

7 Jim Bakker in an interview with *Charisma* (February 1997), 48.

8 Hank Hanegraff, *Christianity in Crisis* (Milton Keynes, England: Nelson Word, 1995), 187.

9 Oral Roberts, *Miracle of Seed-Faith* (Tulsa, Okla: Oral Roberts Evangelistic Association, 1970), 11.

10 Ibid., 11.

11 Ibid., 13.

12 Ibid., 30.

13 Peter Elvy, *Buying Time: The Foundations of the Electronic Church* (Essex, England: McCrimmon, 1986), 81.

14 Patti Roberts with Sherry Androns, *Ashes of Gold* (Waco, Texas: Word Books Publisher, 1983).

15 Oral Roberts, presentation at the World Charismatic Conference, Melodyland Christian Center. Anaheim, Cal. (7 August 1992), as quoted by Hank Hanegraaff in *Christianity in Crisis* (Milton Keynes, England, 1995), 198.

16 Oral Roberts, *Miracle of Seed-Faith*, 66.

17 Gloria Copeland, *God's Will is Prosperity* (Tulsa, Okla: Harrison House, 1978), 54.

18 Kenneth Copeland, *The Laws of Prosperity* (Fort Worth, Tex.: Kenneth Copeland Publications, 1974), p.19.

19 Ibid., 98, 101.

20 Gloria Copeland, *God's Will is Prosperity*, 46.

21 Hank Hanegraaff, *Christianity in Crisis*, 200.

22 Ibid., 188.

23 Dan McConnell, *The Promise of Health And Wealth*, 182–183.

24 Ibid., 174.

25 Hank Hanegraaff, *Christianity in Crisis*, 32.

26 I have observed this in Gabriel Oduyemi's Bethel Chapel in Lagos as well as in other churches.

27 David Oyedepo, *Breaking Financial Hardship* (Lagos, Nigeria: Dominion Publishing House, 1995), 81.

28 David Oyedepo, *Covenant Wealth* (Lagos, Nigeria: Dominion Publishing House, 1992), 21.

29 Oyedepo, *Breaking Financial Hardship*, 22.

30 Ibid., 51.

31 David Oyedepo, *Satan Get Lost: Outstanding Breakthroughs in spite of the Devil* (Lagos, Nigeria:

Dominion Publishing House, 1995), 136.
32 Hank Hanegraaff, *Christianity in Crisis*, 351.
33 Ibid., 131.
34 Oyedepo, *Covenant Wealth*, 23.
35 Oyedepo, *Breaking Financial Hardship*, 147.
36 Ibid., 34.
37 Ibid., 107.
38 Stephen D. Eyre, *Defeating the Dragons*, 28.
39 Jim Bakker, *I Was Wrong* (Nashville, Tenn.: Thomas Nelson, 1996).
40 Jim Bakker in an interview with *Charisma* (February 1997), 48.
41 Ibid., 28.
42 Philip Yancey, *Disappointment with God* (Grand Rapids, Mich.; Zondervan, 1998), 165.
43 Wiersbe, 54–55.
44 Kofi Annan, Statement at the inaugural ceremony of the Third United Nations Conference on the Least Developed Countries. Brussels, 14 May 2001.
45 www.mg.co.za/article/2009-09-03-emotions-high-during-idsuicide-funeral
46 "People Smuggling", www.interpol.int/public/thb/peoplesmuggling/default.asp
47 S. J. Schuller, "Conceptions of Christianity in the Context of Tropical Africa: Nigerian Reactions to its Advent', in C. C. Baeta, *Christianity in Tropical Africa* (London: Oxford University Press, 1968,), 220, as cited in Mbiti, *African Religions and Philosophy* (2nd rev. ed; Oxford: Heinemann, 1969), 232.
48 Quoted in Lamin Sanneh, *Disciples of All Nations: Pillars of World Christianity* (London: Oxford University Press, 2008), 122.
49 Sanneh, *Disciples of All Nations*, 122.
50 "After the Quake", *The Week*, (London, 17 July 2010, Issue 775), 8.
51 "Statistic of the Week", *The Week*, (London, 17 July 2010, Issue 775), 21.
52 "Another £6bn for Goldman bankers", *Daily Mail*, London, July 2010.
53 Ibid.
54 John Stott, *Issues Facing Christians Today* (London: Marshall Pickering, 1990), 246.

Chapter 9. The God Man Uses

1 Femi B. Adeleye, "The God Man Uses" as published in the *National Link* (NIFES Newsletter, Jan-Mar. 1992).
2 In gross misinterpretation of Isaiah 45:11 (KJV).
3 A. W. Tozer, *The Root of the Righteous* (Camp Hill, Penn: Christian Publications, 1955), 11.
4 J. I. Packer, *Knowing God* (Downers Grove; InterVarsity Press, 1973), 6.
5 Ibid., 22.

6 Warren W. Wiersbe, *The Integrity Crisis* (Nashville; Oliver Nelson, 1988), 52.

7 Evelyn Underhill, *Worship* (London: Nisbet, 1936).

8 A. W. Tozer, "Worship: The Missing Jewel of the Evangelical Church", as quoted in *The Best of Tozer* (Grand Rapids, Michigan: Baker, 1978), 217.

Chapter 10. Phoney Christianity

1 Interview reported in *His* magazine (April 1995).

2 Hugh McCullum, *The Angels Have Left Us* (Geneva: WCC, 1995), 41.

3 George Kinoti and Peter Kimuyu, *Vision for a Bright Africa* (Kampala and Nairobi: IFES and AISRED, 1997), 7.

Chapter 11. Authentic Christianity

1 George Kinoti and Peter Kimuyu, *Vision for a Bright Africa* (Kampala and Nairobi: IFES and AISRED, 1997), 9.